AF540278

DPH SPORTS SERIES

SOFTBALL

H. C. DUBEY

1999

DISCOVERY PUBLISHING HOUSE

New Delhi-110002

First Published – 1999

Reprinted – 2026

ISBN: 978-81-7141-483-3

Softball

Published by:

DISCOVERY PUBLISHING HOUSE

4383/4B, Ansari Road, Darya Ganj

New Delhi-110 002 (India)

Phone: +91-11-23279245; 23253475; 43596065

Mobile: +91 9811179893 / +91 9871656464

E-mail: discoverybooksindia@gmail.com

orderdphbooks@gmail.com

namitwasan9@gmail.com

web: www.discoverypublishinggroup.com

Printed at:

Infinity Imaging Systems

Delhi

PREFACE

The need of having a sports series felt because today's situation of the world is not conducive to peace, all round there is destruction, despair, conflict and war; war if not between two nations then within the country itself. In a world where there are some 820 million people unemployed or under-employed, and where 86 million people are born every year, it is not surprising that one out of every four individuals lives in absolute poverty. The *Discovery Publishing House* by Publishing this series seeks to get positive response as—to means by which sports can promote and propagate peace and international cooperation. Sportsmen form a large identifiable cadre. We visualises a situation where a conscious efforts is made all over the world to train the sportspersons to spread the message of peace and international cooperation. Instead of peace keeping efforts through arms and army, the sportspersons may be used as soldiers of peace in a subtle manner. The effort is to make the realize the contribution of sports as a factor for sustainable development, peace keeping and international cooperation.

In developing countries, sports development cooperation is still in the need of justification and steadfast arguments. Many people ask the question "why invest in sports in developing countries for which water supply, health service and agriculture projects are much better suited? An apt reply to this question may be "for many of the people of a developing country,

Sports is the only 'Sweaty' Leisure-time activity. Sports represents a moment of joy in the midst of hard poverty-stricken and dirty everyday life. Doing sports even makes one's work go more smoothly the next day.

This series will be useful to the sports promoters, organisers, coaches and other persons related or interested in sports.

Editor

CONTENTS

Preface

1. Introduction 1
2. Techniques 11
3. Evaluation 16
4. Fundamental Skills 27
5. Teaching Advanced Skills 77
6. Conditioning 114
7. Class Organisation 122
8. Modified Softball Games 129
9. Competitive Softball 136
10. Rules and Regulations 148

Index 208

1

INTRODUCTION

Teaching Softball provides a comprehensive approach to teaching the skills and strategies of slow and fast-pitch softball. It is designed to serve primarily as a reference for physical education students preparing to teach and/or coach, softball teachers and clinicians, recreational leaders directing softball :activities, and coaches in organized competitive softball programs. Many teachers and coaches lack adequate training and sufficient sources of information to assist their players in attaining maximal skill and enjoyment.

Other instructors tend to perpetuate the theories and techniques which they have personally experienced in classes or competition. Frequently, novice teachers seek methodological assistance in conducting well-organized classes and alleviating attitudinal and safety problems.

Similarly, experienced educators and coaches are constantly searching for new ideas and motivational devices. Recognizing the need for relevant organizational and instructional information, the authors formulated this guidebook to facilitate optimal player participation, skill, and enjoyment. Material to assist the teacher and coach in planning softball facilities and selecting equipment, as well as suggestions for making and caring for equipment.

Numerous conditioning exercises and activities designed to promote strength, flexibility, endurance, speed, and power.

Each exercise is classified according to the components of fitness it promotes and its suitability for class or competitive purposes. Techniques of class organization that facilitate instruction are presented.

The program, objectives, class projects, and techniques for teaching basic offensive and defensive skills and strategies to beginning-level players. Many of the suggested drills were tested in pilot programs and were found helpful in developing skills and creating more effective class sessions.

Objectives, performance descriptions of skills, teaching tips, and projects appropriate for advanced level players are offered. The drills and activities in this chapter require prerequisite skills due to their complexity. Let-up activities and variations of the official game which, because of their adaptability, have proven to be popular in school and recreational settings, are presented.

Equipments

Physical educators and athletic coaches recognize the importance of desirable facilities and equipment in conducting safe and effective programs. Whether designing new facilities or modifying existing fields, teaching and coaching personnel should collaborate with architects and facility administrators. Likewise, teachers and coaches should have knowledge of the proper selection of equipment. Frequently, considerations such as cost, playing regulations, safety, and durability will dictate the type of equipment for a particular situation.

Facilities

A softball diamond needs a smooth playing surface, a level outfield, and proper drainage. If space is available, four softball fields are ideal for a school/ recreational complex. Two fields, providing adequate space and facilitating supervision for a large physical education class, require a layout area of 2.32 acres. Fences are desirable, but not mandatory for school use.

Soil content should be tested prior to field construction. Large amounts of clay prevent proper drainage. A suggested mixture for playing fields is 75 percent soil, 15 percent silt, and 10 percent clay. Fields should drain toward the foul lines with a I percent slope. The best grasses for general purpose fields are bluegrass and bermuda grass.

Ideal maintenance includes annual fertilizing of the grass, frequent repair of damaged areas on the field, installing built-in watering systems, and keeping turf about one and one-half to two inches high. Raking the soil smooths and levels the infield area and helps eliminate the hazards of the "bad bounce." This process generally requires expensive machinery. For proper maintenance, raking must be done regularly and also before each competitive event. Synthetic surfaces reduce maintenance and provide an attractive playing area. However, the synthetics have definite disadvantages. The hard, ruglike surface absorbs heat and causes sliding burns, sore legs, and difficulty in handling hard ground balls. It requires special shoes for play. Furthermore, the initial cost of laying the surface is a major inhibitor for most programs.

Lines may be applied to the fields with paint or chalk. Plastic paint is durable and requires less effort to maintain. On the other hand chalk is cheaper, but requires relining especially during frequent use of the playing field and after rainy weather. Also, it is desirable to freshly, line fields before each official game. Portable backstops and benches are frequently used to convert multipurpose fields into softball fields. Auxiliary facilities include scoreboards, batting cages, drinking fountains, bleachers, and lighting. Storage and maintenance provisions are desirable for competitive play, but not necessary for class use.

In teaching situations, equipment of good quality should be purchased. Considerations for purchasing equipment include accommodating right and left-handed players, and providing equipment appropriate for the size of the participants. In coaching situations, players can have more choice in the selection of bats and gloves.

Purchasing the proper amount of equipment is important to any program and is frequently a problem for inexperienced teachers. A rule of thumb suggests that approximately one-fourth of the gloves and mitts ordered should be left-handed.

The official softball is a 12-inch ball weighing between six and one-fourth and seven ounces. It is composed of a kapok or cork core, wound with cotton, dipped in rubber cement and coated with horsehide. The exterior of the ball is smoothly seamed. When purchasing official balls, the buyer should be sure that all specifications are met. The Amateur Softball Association endorses certain manufacturers' brands, which conform to the association's high standards, and allows the ASA trademark to appear on the ball covers. Differences between brands are generally in size, seam construction, smoothness, and weights; all fall within the standards. Frequently official softballs with slight flaws in the leather are marked "seconds" by manufacturers and may be purchased at sizable discounts.

Generally, the regulation 12-inch ball is preferred for intermediate and advanced players. However, official softballs may not be necessary or desirable for all class purposes. Elementary students may use the fleece balls or rubber playground balls. Twelve or 14-inch "super-soft" or restricted flight balls are appropriate for teaching skills to young and inexperienced players. The softness decreases player fear in fielding batted balls, and permits balls to be caught easily with or without gloves.

The 16-inch ball is popular in secondary and college-level co-recreational leagues and coeducation classes., Primarily used to offset differences in skill, the larger ball also allows advanced players to participate in limited space. One problem with using the larger balls, however, is that inexperienced players have difficulty throwing with sufficient power.

Rubber-covered balls are suggested for damp playing surfaces, thus eliminating the possibility of water-saturated balls. Although quite durable, these balls are harder than those covered with leather.

Ideally, each player should have a properly fitting

glove of good quality. The glove is an important teaching and learning aid, as it protects the hand and reduces the player's fear of injury. The school or recreation department should attempt to provide gloves for all players whenever feasible. If the department cannot afford to purchase gloves, players should be encouraged to bring their own. Whenever personal items are used in class, certain precautions should be taken to protect the equipment from loss or theft. Students should print their names with indelible ink inside their gloves. Personal equipment should be stored in personal lockers or checked in and out of the equipment room. Teachers may approach recreational teams, individuals, or business people in the community to obtain new or discarded gloves suitable for class use. Fund-raising projects may provide another means of obtaining equipment.

The official rules distinguish between glove and mitt construction. Mitts, gloves without separate fingers, are permitted for the catcher and first baseman only. The first baseman's mitt is more flexible and less padded than the catcher's mitt. For slow-pitch softball, catchers may use a regular glove. Before purchasing any gloves, several styles should be tested for pocket suitability and leather pliability.

In the interest of safety, the catcher should be required to wear a face mask and body protector during class play. Although not required by all official softball rules, this equipment is also recommended for recreational play and athletic competition. Certainly the wearing of a catcher's mask should be a minimal requirement for any player behind the plate.

In order to accommodate individual needs and preferences, a variety of bats should be available. Selections should include different weights and grip sizes. Bats may not exceed 34 inches in length and must have a safety grip. Most wooden bats are composed of northern white ash, while most metal bats are aluminum. Generally speaking, one bat for every five players will suffice for instructional purposes. Competitive teams may desire at least 20 bats to allow for breakage and to offer players a choice of weight and grip sizes. Players may also have preferences regarding the shape and style of the bat. Some bats are bottle shaped with the weight distribution close to the center; others are thin and tapered with the weight closer to the end. Shorter bats, with more mass in the hitting portion, are recommended for beginners. For liability and safety reasons, all bats should be checked daily for breaks, and discarded, not taped, if any breaks are discovered. For competitive players desiring additional traction, shoes with metal or rubber cleats may be purchased in a variety of styles. Special rubber-cleated shoes are available for play on synthetic surfaces. Although the rubber cleats reduce the chance of injury to others, they do not offer the footing that the metal cleat provides. It should be noted that metal cleats may not be legal for high school competition and are not recommended for class play.

A competitive team should be outfitted in numbered uniforms of identical color and style which comply with league regulations. In addition, the governing association may require batting helmets for player protection.

After purchasing the essential class or team

equipment, the teacher or coach can reduce program costs by making other desirable items. Ball and bat bags can be made by sewing together heavy pieces of canvas material and inserting a drawstring in a hem sewn across the top. Burlap or feed sacks sewn into one and-a-half foot squares and stuffed with sawdust make adequate bases when anchored to the ground. Resin bags can be similarly made by machine or hand.

Yarn wound into balls can be used by beginners for indoor skill practice and novelty games. Portable and permanent bat racks may be constructed for use on the playing field and in the equipment room.

A batting tee can be constructed from the following materials:

1. One 1 x 12-inch base board, preferably with the end cut in the shape of home plate
2. One 1 x 10-inch top board about 10-inches in length
3. One pipe flange
4. One piece of 1¼ inch water pipe approximately 30-36 inches long with six holes drilled three inches apart starting at one end of the pipe
5. One piece of corded radiator hose, capable of sliding up and down over the water pipe
6. One nail
7. Four to six 1¼ inch screws

The steps in constructing the batting tee are:

1. Nail the flat top board to the center of the base board.
2. With screws, attach the pipe flange to the center of the top board.

3. Screw the water pipe into the flange with the holes at the bottom end of the pine
4. Slide the hose down over the top of the pipe, with the drilled holes exposed below the hose.
5. Insert the nail in one of the holes to act as a stopper for the hose. The selection of holes allows the batter to adjust the hose up and down the pipe to a preferred height.

Scoreboards may be as simple as a chalkboard, with innings marked off in paint and attachable plates, or as elaborate as a lighted scoreboard. The former may be constructed easily and 'placed in a visible, out of bounds location along one sideline or in deep center field.

Care of equipment

Gloves

Gloves may be cleaned with leather-cleaning products or with saddle soap and a small amount of water. To keep the leather supple and retain the desired shape of the glove, neatsfoot oil may be applied and a ball placed in the pocket. A string is wrapped around the glove tightly to support the ball in this position.

Balls

Leather balls may be cleaned of mud, dirt, and grass stain by using saddle soap or a ball cleaner. Rubber-covered balls can be washed with soap and water.

Bats

Bats should be cleaned thoroughly following practices and games. A light oil should be applied periodically to prevent drying of wooden bats. Aluminum bats may be wiped off with a damp cloth and mild soap.

Cracked or Split bats should be discarded. No attempt should be made to repair broken bats. However, rough areas may be sanded and grips may be replaced. Bat handles must be, checked for loose or unraveling tape. For storage, bats may be hung from bat racks or stored flat on shelves.

Shoes

When leather shoes are damp from wet playing surfaces, stuffing with paper and drying at room temperature maintains the shape. Oil applied to the leather tops and soles of the shoes helps prevent cracking. Canvas shoes can be washed with lukewarm water and soap. Laces and cleats should be checked before each practice and game and repaired if necessary. Insoles may be sprayed with disinfectant or powdered to prevent athlete's foot.

2

TECHNIQUES

Developed from baseball via the indoor version of that game, softball is a comparatively young sport that, perhaps surprisingly, enjoys an even greater international following than its parent. While the rules of the two games differ considerably, the only major difference in techniques lies in the method of pitching. Unlike baseball, where the ball is pitched with anything from an overarm to a sidearm action, in softball the rules require that the ball must be delivered with an underarm action. Since the other techniques used in softball have already been analyzed in the chapter on baseball, the discussion in this present chapter is confined to an analysis of pitching.

Techniques

Pitching

Stance. In taking the initial position on the rubber, the pitcher places the feet approximately shoulder width apart with the heel of the right shoe in contact with the front half of the rubber and the toe of the left shoe in contact with the back half. This position of the feet provides a relatively broad base and therefore reasonable stability; it affords the opportunity to obtain the maximum distance through which to exert force on the ball; and last, but not least, it conforms with the rules. Having carefully placed the feet in the required position, the pitcher assumes an erect stance with the center of gravity directly over the left foot. Both hands are held in front at, or slightly below, waist height with the ball concealed in the glove.

Delivery. The two main methods of delivery are:

1. the *windmill*, in which the pitcher's arm rotates through approximately 360° in a vertical or near-vertical plane before the ball is released.
2. the *slingshot*, in which the pitcher's arm is moved backward and somewhat towards first base, until it is "above the head and nearly perpendicular to the ground" before being brought forward again to the point where the ball is released.

While only the former is considered in this chapter, it should be noted that many of the points made apply equally well to both methods of delivery. The wind-up preceding the release of the ball begins with the pitcher moving both hands downward and forward to a position near the knees. This movement draws the shoulders forward and, aided by a slight flexing of the knees, serves to set the center of gravity moving in a forward and downward direction. Once the hands have reached the low point of their downward motion, the pitcher pushes against the rubber with the left foot and then brings the left leg forward .and upward in unison with a forward and upward swing of the arms. As a result of these actions the pitcher's center of gravity moves forward of the right foot and into a position from which moments later a forceful extension of the right leg drives it still farther in a forward and upward direction.

During the course of these striding movements the arms continue forward and upward until they are roughly horizontal, at which stage the right arm continues its backward rotation while the left one remains where it is and assists in maintaining the required balance. As the right arm swings overhead and begins to descend, the pitcher's body turns so that the hips and trunk face sideways. This action serves two main purposes:

1. It places the body in a position where the muscles responsible for hip and trunk rotation can make a contribution to the speed of the ball at release.
2. It increases the distance through which the ball may be accelerated.

The stride is completed when the heel of the left foot strikes the ground some 1.5-1.8 in from the rubber and slightly to the left of the intended line of the pitch. This off-line placement of the foot permits the hips to be fully rotated to the front and thus make a maximal contribution to the speed of the ball at release. After the left heel has landed, the rest of the foot is quickly grounded and the hip, knee, and ankle joints of the left leg flex to reduce the force of the impact.

Once the left foot has been grounded, the pitcher's body rotates to the front, partly due to the eccentric ground reaction evoked and partly as a result of the internal muscular forces exerted at that time. This rotation of the body brings the right shoulder forward and causes the path followed by the ball to be "flattened out" as it approaches the point of release.

Release. Once the point of release has been reached, the centripetal force exerted on the ball by the pitcher's hand is removed. Then, no longer restrained in this manner, the ball flies off in the direction it was moving at the instant of release (that is, in a direction tangential to its path at the point of release). Because the direction in which the ball is moving as it leaves the pitcher's hand largely determines the ultimate success of a pitch, the point at which the ball is released is obviously of critical importance. If it is released before it reaches the correct (or optimum) point, it is likely to be lower than intended as it passes over the plate. Similarly, if the release takes place at some point beyond the optimum, the ball is likely to be higher than intended.

The flattening of the path followed by the ball during the latter stages of the delivery affords the pitcher some room for error in the point of release. For, with such a flattened path, a point of release that deviates slightly from the optimum produces a less marked difference in the direction in which the ball is released than would be the case if the ball's path were a true circular arc. Thus, the flattening of the path followed by the ball is not only an indication that the hip and trunk rotations have been correctly executed but, because it permits some latitude in the point of release, is also of value in itself.

The height at which the ball should be released, relative to the pitcher's body, depends on a number of factors, including the speed of the ball as it is released and that point in the strike zone (high or low) at which it is desired to place it. In general, however, the optimum point of release lies somewhere between knee and hip height.

Follow-through. The follow-through after the release of the ball serves exactly the same purposes in softball as it does in baseball--namely, to reduce the speed of the various body parts (and in particular, the pitching arm) without risk of injury and without impairing the application of forces to the ball.

Once the follow-through is completed, the pitcher moves quickly into position to field the ball should it be hit in his (or her) direction. This need to move quickly into a fielding position is heightened by the fact that the pitching rubber is only 14.02 m from the plate (compared with 18.44 m in baseball) and the pitcher thus has even less time before the ball can be returned than does his (or her) baseball counterpart.

3

EVALUATION

In an educational setting, evaluation of psychomotor and cognitive competencies should be an integral part of the teaching process. Most evaluative procedures only measure the performance at the time of testing and not potential performance. Therefore periodic evaluation is desirable in determining the student's progression and improvement. Repeated evaluations may also serve as practice sessions and motivational devices, thus making instruction more meaningful, Pretests are valuable in obtaining basic information for later comparisons. To determine improvement, periodic or post-unit tests render feedback regarding instructional effectiveness.

Various measurement techniques may be employed to determine a player's success in meeting desired personal and group objectives. To evaluate skill and knowledge levels, three appropriate instruments skill tests, rating scales, and knowledge tests are frequently applied. In selecting tests suitable for evaluating performance in a given situation, several criteria should be considered, such as validity, reliability, scoring method, degree of difficulty, and administrative feasibility. The authors recommend the following tests for skill assessment.

The American Alliance for Health, Physical Education, Recreation and Dance endorsed eight comprehensive tests of softball skills and provided national performance norms for ages 10 to 18. Seven of these tests appear below. Based upon the twentieth percentile scores for each age group and sex, a performance expectancy chart has been designed to accompany these tests. Performance scores charted for ages 7 to 12 provide minimal acceptable expectations for beginning level players. Expectations for 13 to 15-year-olds suggest minimal, intermediate level skill standards. Scores for the age range of 16 to 18 offer lower limit expectations for the advanced level players.

Regarding the administration of these tests, student assistants may be trained in the techniques of testing when employing a station to station procedure.

Skill tests

1. *Throw for distance.* Measures the distance a softball can be thrown.

   Equipment. A smooth grass or dirt field with throwing-zone lines marked, softballs, measuring tape, and stake markers.

   Description. Mark off a zone six feet wide from which the throw must be made. One or two steps may be taken preceding the throw. The player throws three balls at right angles to the throwing line. Mark the point at which the first ball hits the ground. If the second or third throw is farther, mark the new point. It speeds up measuring if, after three consecutive throws, the player stands at the furthest mark. After four or five players have thrown, all their distances can be measured at the same time. Players must be warmed up before throwing. Throws must be measured at right angles to the throwing line and to the nearest measured foot. The distance of the best throw should be recorded on the squad scorecard.

2. Overhand throw for accuracy. Measures the accuracy of a throw from the approximate distance of an infielder's throw to a base or home plate.

   Equipment: A smooth wall on which a target can be placed, or a target marked on the wall; softballs, measuring tape, chalk.

   Description: The target consists of three concentric circles, marked by lines one inch wide, painted on an area at least eight feet square. A wall, or a canvas or mat hung on the wall, may be used. The center circle is two feet in diameter, and the outer circle six feet in diameter. The bottom of the outer circle is three feet above the floor, The throw is made from behind a line parallel to, and 65 feet from, the target. After one or two practice throws, the player throws ten times. Both feet must be behind the fine at the time of the throw, but the player may take one or two steps before making the throw.

   Scoring. Balls hitting in the center circle count three points; in the middle area, count two points; and in the outer area count one point. Balls hitting on a line count as the higher number of points. The score is the sum of points made on ten throws. Record points as each throw is made. The maximum score is 30 points.

3. *Underhand pitching*. Measures the accuracy with which a softball can be pitched. Equipment. A gymnasium or outdoor space adjacent to a smooth wall, target, softballs, measuring.

   Description. A rectangular target with an inner rectangle 17 inches wide and 30 inches high, and an outer rectangle which is six inches larger on all sides, is painted on canvas or marked on a wall. The lines are one inch wide. The target is placed so that the bottom of the outer rectangle is 18 inches above the floor. A pitching line 24 inches long is marked 46 feet from the target and parallel to it. The player is allowed one practice pitch and then takes 15 underhand pitches.

   One foot must be kept on the pitching line while delivering the ball. A forward step can be taken while making the pitch. Illegal pitches should not be scored.

   Scoring. Pitched balls hitting in the center area, or on its boundary line, count two points; in the outer area, or on its outside boundary tine, count one point. The score is the sum of all points made on 15 pitches. The maximum score is 30 points.

4. *Speed throw*. Measures the speed with which a player can handle the ball in catching and throwing.

   Equipment. A gymnasium or a smooth ground surface, softballs, stopwatch.

   Description. A line is drawn on the floor or ground, nine feet from, and parallel to, a smooth wall eight to ten feet in width arid height. From behind the line, the player throws the ball overhand against the wall, and catches the rebound as rapidly as possible. This is repeated for 15 throws. For best results, the ball should hit the wall at the height of, or a bit above, the thrower. Players start on the signal "go," but time is started when the ball hits the wall. Balls which fall short can be retrieved, but the player must return and throw from behind the line One new trial may be given if the ball gets entirely away from the player. After a practice trial two trials are timed with the best time counted as the score.

Scoring. The score is the time in seconds, and tenths of seconds, required for the 15 consecutive hits on the wall. Time starts when the first ball hits the wall arid stops as the fifteenth throw hits the wall. Both times are recorded on the squad scorecard.

5. *Fungo hitting.* Measures the skill with which a player can hit fly balls alternately to right field and left field.

   Equipment: A standard softball diamond and field with baselines marked arid bases in position; softball bats of several weights, softballs.

   Description: The player stands behind home plate with a bat and a ball in hand. The first attempted fungo hit is a fly ball to right field, The next attempt is a fly ball into left field. Alternately hitting to the right and left is continued until ten hits are attempted to each side (a total of 20 hits). The score is recorded as each ball is hit and the sums of the 20 hits are counted as the score. Two balls missed entirely, in succession, count as an attempt. The tester may call "right" or "left" to indicate the side to which the next hit is to be hit. Practice trials to each side are allowed, Scoring. Fly balls which land beyond the baseline on the intended side count two points, while ground balls hit across the baseline on the intended side count one point. Foul balls and balls settling in the infield count zero points. When hits intended for right field land at the left of second base, no score is made. Similarly when balls intended for left field go to the right of second base, no score is made. The maximum score is 40 points.

6. *Baserunning.* Measures the speed with which a player can run around the bases after a swing at an imaginary pitch.

   Equipment. A standard softball field and diamond with home plate, bases, and a batter's box laid out for a right-handed batter; softball bats, stopwatch.

   Description. The player takes position in the right-hand batter's box, holding a bat as if ready for a pitch. On the signal "hit" the player takes a complete swing at an imaginary ball, drops the bat (it must not be thrown), and runs around the bases, being careful to touch each base. A practice run is allowed. Two trials are recorded and the best score is counted. The trials are timed in seconds and tenths of seconds from the signal "hit," to the instant the runner touches home plate after circling the bases.

7. *Fielding ground balls.* Measures the ability of a player to field ground balls quickly. Equipment. A smooth area on which markings can be placed, softballs, baskets, a sweep-hand watch, measuring tape, marking equipment.

Description. An area 17 by 60 feet is marked on a field. A throwing line is designated at one end. Two lines are drawn in this area, a line 50 feet from the throwing line and the other 25 feet from the throwing line. The player being tested stands inside the ten-foot area beyond the 50-foot line. An assistant with the basket of ten balls stands behind the throwing line. Spare balls are available if needed. On signal "go," the assistant throws grounders into the marked area at five-second intervals. Each throw must strike the ground, for at least one bounce, between the throwing line and the 25-foot line and be within the side lines. The thrower should throw overhand with good speed, like a machine, with some variation in direction, but not trying to make the fielder miss. A throw not made as specified can be repeated. The player must field each ball cleanly, hold it momentarily, toss it aside, and then prepare for the next ball. The player starts behind the 50-foot line but thereafter fields anywhere behind the 25-foot fine. If a series of throws is interrupted, it may be repeated at the discretion of the tester. A practice trial is allowed.

Scoring. Each ball correctly fielded counts one point. Record a point or a zero for each throw. The score is the total of points on 20 throws; the maximum score is 20 points.

8. *Catching fly balls.* Measures skill in catching at frequent intervals. In testing beginners, the balls should be thrown. However, for intermediate and advanced players the balls may be thrown or batted.

Description. The student being tested stands approximately 60 feet from the tosser who has a ball in hand and a supply of balls within reach. On the signal "go" given by the tester, the tosser makes overhand throws of approximately 30 feet in height to the player. The player must catch each ball and then toss or roll it to a catcher standing beside the tosser. The tosser continues to throw at ten-second intervels.

9. *Repeated throws.'* Measures a player's ability to catch an aerial ball and make a rapid throw. This is similar to the test for fielding ground balls. A restraining line is drawn 23 feet from a smooth wall, and a line is drawn on the wall ten feet frorn the floor and parallel to it.

   Description. The player stands behind the restraining line, facing the wall, with a ball in the throwing hand. On the signal "go," the player throws the ball overhand or sidearm at the wall, so that it strikes above the ten-foot line, and`then catches the return as it comes off the wall. The player repeats the process as rapidly as possible. Each throw must be madè from behind the 23-foot line. Any mishandled ball must be recovered before the next throw. A practice trial precedes each of the four 30-second trials. For each ball that is thrown from behind the 23-foot line and strikes the wall above the ten-foot line, a point is scored. Points totalled for all four trials. Suggested minimal skill performances are as follows:

10. *The batting tee test.* Suitable for assessing the beginners' ability to hit squarely a stationary ball for distance. (Batting form may be subjectively

evaluated while testing.) In preparation for the test, mark off 15 parallel lines, each five yards apart on an open playing area. A batting tee is placed in the middle of the first line,

Description. The batter assumes a normal batting stance and hits a ball off the tee as far as possible, Five practice trials are allowed, followed by 20 trials for score. 'Fite distance is measured to the nearest yard from the too to the point where each ball first lands, The recorded score is a total of the distances for the '20 trials presently norms are not available as indicators of minimal skill performance.

11. *Batting pitched balls.* Recommended as one instrument for determining a player's ability to hit a pitched ball into fair territory. Unless, a pitching machine is used to provide uniformity in every pitch, the teacher must recognize/c possibility of a loss of reliability in the test. However, when using a player for pitching purposes, it is suggested to have the same pitcher throw similar pitches to all tested players, Another alternative is to use two pitchers, administer the test twice, and total both scores.

    Description. The batter stands in the batter's box and is allowed ten trials to hit legal underhand pitches. Strikes may be called by an umpire, if desired, but bans are disregarded. Three points are awarded for balls hit into fair territory, one point is awarded for a foul ball, and no points for strikes (called or missed). The total points for the ten trials are recorded.

The authors choose not to recommend minimal skill performances for this test due to variations in pitches and differences in hitting slow vs,. fast pitched balls. Each instructor is encouraged to establish standards suitable for the situation and skill level of the players involved. Observation of players in practice and game situations is vital in assessing skill technique. Rating scales and checklists contribute objectivity to these observational appraisals. Such lists categorize offensive and defensive skills into their basic components. Furthermore, rating scales allow the observer to designate the level of proficiency in executing each skill.

Game statistics may offer the instructor valuable information regarding a student's application of garne skills, In assessing the player's "total" skill performance, consideration should be given to several individual statistics, including batting averages, errors, stolen bases, strike-outs, sacrifice flies, bases on balls, etc. As the skill level of the class increases, statistical information can be used to a greater extent for evaluative purposes. Students should be familiarized with each statistical category as the corresponding rules are introduced.

Proper scorekeeping techniques can be taught and practiced in class. Players unable to actively participate may be involved in the game as scorers and statisticians.

In addition to reports and class discussions student achievement of the cognitive objectives for the softball unit may be objectively determined through the use of written quizzes and examinations. Knowledge tests should reflect the cognitive competencies desired for all players of that level. Ambiguous questions which allow for variance of interpretation should be eliminated. Well constructed, teacher-made tests may be more relevant and suitable to the situation than standardized tests. The content of each 'examination should correspond to the knowledge and skill progressions taught.

4

FUNDAMENTAL SKILLS

The purpose of this chapter is to present information that will aid in teaching novice players the fundamental skills of catching, throwing, batting, and baserunning. In determining the content appropriate for beginning players, the leader should give careful attention to each player's ability and attitude. Some players have limited experience or ability but great enthusiasm for softball; while other players may have had experiences which cause them to fear the game emotionally, physically, or both. The leader should try to avoid placing the beginning player in situations which might be frustrating or embarrassing. Provisions should be made for learning experiences that are meaningful and fun,

For a unit of instruction to be meaningful, the teacher must have in mind particular goals and expectations for the student, Likewise, realistic objectives and a knowledge of how achievement will be determined may serve to motivate and direct the student. Performance objectives, commonly referred to as "behavioral objectives," are "specific statements of proposed educational outcomes."[1] The "specificity" refers to the three criteria which distinguish behavioral objectives from their more ambiguous counterparts.

First, a behavioral objective must describe the exact performance, such as, the student will be able to properly execute, an overhand softball throw. Second, the minimum performance must be designated, such as, the student will be, able to properly execute an overhand softball throw a distance of 75 feet. Third, the behavioral objective must define how the performance will be evaluated, such as, the student will he able to properly execute an overhand softball, throw a distance of 75 feet at least once in three trials. The explicit and unambiguous terminology, which characterizes behavioral objectives, gives the reader a clear under-standing of the desired performances and their measurement.

The cognitive domain encompasses knowledge comprehension, application, analysis, synthesis, and evaluation. In softball, the student must be able to apply these processes to learning the rules, techniques, and strategies of the game. Achievement of the objectives in this domain could be determined through observation of the student's performance in various game situations, or through discussion and written testing for understanding.

Objectives appropriate for the psychomotor domain involve specific motor and fitness skills. In a softball unit, the development of such skill as throwing, catching, batting, base running, and fielding are the "expected performances" of the psychomotor behavioural objectives. Acceptable evaluative techniques for this domain include observation, skill testing, and performance charting. Motivating students of various abilities to practice new skills arid improve existing competencies is a challenge for any instructor,

Many teachers have difficulty, in determining measurable performance objectives in the affective domain, which relate to feelings, attitudes, values arid appreciations. Inherent to all instruction in physical education is the development of such desirable student qualities as leadership, sportsmanship, an improved self-image and value system, sensitivity to others, and adherance to the rules of play. In teaching a softball unit instructor may wish to promote positive attitudes and expressions through affective behavioral objectives. For example, students should be encouraged to demonstrate in game situations respect for official's calls by accepting all decisions and addressing the official in a courteous manner. Once such objectives are determined, for the group, participants should be encouraged to assist their peers in achieving the goals Sensitivity to others, honesty, and the ability to be a team player are observable qualities which rnay carry over into other aspects of the student's life.

To enhance achievement in all three domains, the teacher should provide learning experiences which afford opportunities for development and individualized instruction. The text attempts to suggest some appropriate student" activities in the form of drills, lead-up games, and projects which appear in this and subsequent chapters.

Cognitive objectives

As a result of participating hi this unit the student will:

1. Demonstrate a knowledge of the game and rules of softball by attaining a minimum grade of 70 percent on the written comprehensive examination for beginning level players.

2. Demonstrate through performance a knowledge of the duties and skills for each position on the field, and a basic understanding of the concept of team play.
3. Demonstrate cognitive knowledge of history, terminology and safety precautions through written reports, class discussions, and satisfactory performance by obtaining a minimum grade of 70 percent on the written examination.

Psychomotor objectives

As a result of participating in this unit the student will

1. Properly execute an underhand throw from a distance of 40 feet at moderate pace.
2. Properly execute an overhand throw from a distance of 90 feet (males) or 45 feet (females) which must reach the target baseman without bouncing
3. Properly catch high, low, and ground balls thrown overhand from a distance of 50 feet as determined by the instructor's appraisal.
4. Bat a teed softball and a slowly pitched ball, using good form as determined by the instructor's appraisal.
5. Be able to meet minimum skill performance levels for the appropriate age group on each of the softball skill tests.

As a result of participation in this unit the student will:

1. Demonstrate an interest in the game by participating in practice and games during leisure time.

2. Demonstrate adherence to the rules of the game during competition.

3. Demonstrate positive interpersonal relationship by supporting and encouraging others.

When fielding, a player will have to catch thrown balls, ground balls, and fly balls. To catch hardhit balls and balls bit to either side of, and away from, the fielder, the player must use additional skills which involve getting into the proper position. Beginners should be taught to effectively wear and use the glove.

Catching without a glove

Learning to catch without a glove allows the beginner to better conceptualize the fundamentals of catching: watching the ball, relaxing the fingers, catching with both hands, and "giving" with the ball.

Performance description

I. Watch the ball throughout its flight.

2. Position the hands and body in line with the path of the ball.

3. For bails chest high or higher, position the hands so the thumbs are close together and the fingers pointed upward. For balls waist high and lower, position the hand with the little fingers close together and the fingers pointed downward.

4. Extend the hands and arms toward the ball.

5. Open the hands and relax the fingers and arms.

6. Watch the ball come into the hands.

7. Absorb the force of the ball with both hands by giving with the hands, arms, and body.

Common errors

1. Failure to relax the fingers and hands.
2. Closing the eyes or turning the head on impact.

Teaching tips and strategy

1. Softer and larger balls may be used when initially teaching catching.
2. Players should begin tossing and catching at close range.
3. The distance may be increased as players gain confidence.

Drills

To overcome fear in catching, the drills of "toss up" and "clap catch" may be used. From these self-paced drills the player may progress to throwing the ball against a wall, thus learning to judge the angle and speed of the ball,

Toss-up. Each player has a bail. The player tosses the ball into the air and catches it. The player should be encouraged to toss the ball as high as possible and still be able to catch it.

Clap catch. As players gain confidence in tossing the ball up in the air and catching it, a variation can be introduced in which the player claps the hands together one or more times while the ball is in the air. Players are encouraged to increase the number of claps by tossing the ball higher. Thus the player learns to judge the height of the ball and becomes accustomed to balls that are travelling a greater distance. If desired, players can compete to execute the most claps.

Catching with a glove

Just prior to teaching the overhand throw, the proper use of the glove should be taught. The glove increases the likelihood of the bail being caught and reduces the chances of injury.

Performance description

I. Place the fingers comfortably in the glove.
2. Watch the ball from the moment of the throw or hit.
3. Move quickly to a position in line with the flight of the ball.
4. Place the body and the glove in the proper position. The glove position depends on the trajectory of the ball as described in catching without a glove.
S. Extend the hands and arms toward the ball.
6. Open the hands and glove. Relax the fingers.
7. Watch the ball come into the glove.
8. Catch with both hands.
9. Allow the hands and glove to fold or close around the ball.
10. "Give" with the ball with hands, arms, and body.
11. Prepare to throw by bringing the ball to the throwing position.

Common errors

1. Improper use of the glove. Closing the glove too soon.
2. Failure to catch with both hands.

Teaching tips and strategy

1. Confidence in catching fly balls may be developed by initially catching thrown balls from a short distance, and later increasing the distance and trajectory of the ball.

2. When teaching the correct method of using a glove, special emphasis should be given to opening the glove, allowing the ball to come into the glove, and closing the glove around the ball, "Let the glove do the work" is a good motto to adopt.

3. The glove should feel as though it is a natural part of the hand. This is best achieved by wearing the glove and catching with it as much as possible. Many teachers and coaches insist that players wear their gloves while they run laps or do footwork drills.

4. The presence of the glove does not reduce the importance of relaxing the fingers, catching with two hands, and giving with the ball. The use of the throwing hand aids in the catch and in preparation for a quick throw. As the ball enters the glove, the throwing hand traps the ball to keep it in the glove and initiate the throw.

5. Beginners often demonstrate a tendency to get the throwing hand in the way, or to try to catch the ball with the throwing hand. In order to avoid injury, these players should be given individualized attention and drilled on the proper mechanics.

In the early stages of learning, the target for the catch should be made by holding the glove at approximately shoulder height, slightly toward the throwing side of the body. This glove position causes fewer movements in preparation for the throw when the player is going to return the ball quickly. Also, the habit of throwing to a target helps insure that the ban is not thrown to someone who is not looking. "Do not throw the ball unless the fielder has made a target" should be constant warning to the players.

Drills

Since throwing and catching are practiced simultaneously, the drills listed for throwing practice are appropriate for both.

The underhand throw is used to pitch the ball to the batter or toss it gently, to a nearby fielder. Beginning players should practice the skill of pitching as much as possible. The fun and excitement of the game is thwarted when the pitcher cannot get the ball over the plate for the batters to hit. Fielders use the overhand throw when throwing the ball long distances to other fielders or basemen.

Introducing the underhand pitch or throw before teaching tire overhand throw has several advantages.

1. It allows a longer practice time for a skill that often is insufficiently developed.
2. During the early practice and drill sessions it may help players overcome the fear of catching a ball that is thrown overhand.
3. The player achieves success with the underhand throw before becoming involved with the complex mechanics of the overhand throw,

Performance description

I. Using a tripod or four-finger grip, hold the ball in front of the body.

2. Face the target. The foot on non-throwing side of the body is even with, or slightly behind, the foot on the throwing side of the body.
3. Bring the ball down and back in semicircular backswing. The arm straightens and the wrist cocks at the end of the backswing.,
4. Step forward on the opposite foot and swing the arm forward in a pendular motion.
5. Snap the wrist, release the ball from the fingertips at the 8 o'clock position with a lifting motion.
6. Follow through, step forward on tire throwing side foot, and assume the fielding position

Common errors

I. Holding the ball on the palm of the hand.
2. Insufficient backswing.
3. Improper timing on release
4. Lack of transfer of weight,
5. Insufficient follow through.
6. Failure to assume fielders Position.

Teaching Tips and Strategy

1. Initially, beginning players should stress accuracy in pitching the ball into the strike zone. Factors such as speed, are, and spin should be introduced only after control is apparent.
2. The pitching skill may be practiced by having the players work in groups of three: a pitcher, a catcher, and batter. The batter does not attempt to bat the ball but assumes the batting stance. Having

the batter present gives the pitcher a better perspective of the strike zone, and provides a better target area.

Although the underhand throw is the first stage in the development of throwing skills, the player should progress to the overhand throw as quickly as possible. Allowing the player to use the underhand throw exclusively for too long a period may deter or prolong the development of the overhand throw.

4. For safety and defensive reasons, strong emphasis must be placed on the pitcher assuming a balanced fielding position after the pitch.
5. The grip will vary according, to the pitcher's hand size and ability to control the ball. The grip should be comfortable for the pitcher.
6. When using the underhand motion, as a toss to a baseman who is in close range, the backswing is generally shorter and the ball is gently tossed to the player.
7. For both the underhand toss and Pitch, emphasize a "lifting" motion and rolling the ball off the fingertips.
8. In slow pitch pitching, the pitcher should take several quick steps backward after the release of the ball. This puts the pitcher in a good fielding position in front of second base.

Target pitching. The pitcher practices by pitching the ball at, the target on a wall or through a frame which designates the strike zone.

Slow pitch drill. Stretch a clothesline between two poles at a height of nine feet. From a distance of 46 feet, a pitcher practices arching the ball over the line to a catcher. Option: a backstop may bused instead of the clothesline.

Overhand throw

The overhand throw may be described as a unilateral overarm motion in which the elbow swings forward ahead of the forearm and the forearm extends prior to the release.' The overhand throw is a basic skill for all positions. Proper development of the ovehand throw allows the Player the ball with more velocity and accuracy than any other for distance.

Performance description

I. Hold the ball in the fingers with a tripod grip or four-fingered grip.

2. Pivot on the throwing side foot, pointing the opposite hip, side and shoulder toward the target. At the same time bring the ball to a position above the shoulder at approximately ear height with the wrist cocked back. The tipper arm is parallel to the ground and away from the body.

3. Step toward the target with the front foot. Simultaneously, rotate tile body toward the target in the following sequence: hips, trunk, shoulders.

4. Begin the forward swing of the arm by leading with the elbow.

5. With a snap of the wrist, release the ball from the finger tips.

6. Follow through toward the target, letting the arm come to rest near the hip on the non-throwing side.

Common errors

I. Holding the ball in the palm of the hand.

2. Facing the target rather than pivoting.

3. Keeping the upper arm close to the body,

4. Failure to transfer the weight and rotate the body.

S. Failure to snap the wrist,

6. Failure to follow through.

Teaching tips and strategy

I. Beginning players should start throwing and catching at a close range and gradually increase the distance and height of the throw.

2. Regardless of the distance the ball is thrown, the skill should be properly executed.

3. It is often helpful to compare the motion of the overhand throw to that of snapping a whip. Letting players actually "crack" a rope in a whiplike fashion may help them with this motion.

4. For long throws, players should take a couple of step-hops toward the target in preparation for the throw.

Drills

Two-player throw. Practicing proper fundamentals, two players face each other, form targets with gloves and throw.

Three-player throw. Three players form a linc, with players on the ends facing the middle player. Each player forms a target with the glove. Player number I throws the ball to player number 2. Player number 2 pivots on the glove-side and throws to player number

3. Fielding grounders may be added by having player number 2 toss ground balls to the two end players. The end players throw the ball back to the middle player.

Four-player throw. Four player throw is basically the same as three-player throw except one player is added.

Fielding ground balls

Infielders and outfielders need constant practice in fielding ground balls. Practice should cover fielding balls to the right and left, requiring the players to use the slide and crossover steps.

Performance description

1. Assume a ready position with the feet parallel, weight forward, knees and hips flexed and the hands close to the ground.
2. As the ball is hit, move to a position in the path of the ball, keeping the body and glove low. If possible, move toward or "charge" the ball. If the ball is within two or three steps to either side of the fielder, a slide step is used. The slide step consists on a step-close-step, starting with the foot closest to the ball.
3. Once in line with the ball, bend the hips and knees in order to get the hands and body low to the ground.
4. If the ball is several steps away, pivot on the foot closest to the ball, cross over with the opposite foot and move toward the ball.
5. Shift the body weight forward.
6. For routine ground balls, extend the arms toward the ball, and properly position the glove, touching

the ground by the inside of the forward foot. Point the fingers to the ground. Field balls on the glove side of the body with the thumb away from the body. Field balls on the non-glove side of the body with the glove in a backhand position.

7. Keep the glove open, the head down and watch the ball enter the glove.
8. As the ball is caught, place the throwing hand over the ball and prepare for the throw.

Common errors

1. Failure to get in the path of the ball.
2. Closing the eyes or turning or lifting the head prior to catching the ball.

Teaching tips and strategy

1. For the beginning players a ball softly thrown is less threatening than a batted ban.
2. Players should be reminded to keep the glove close to the ground and to use the body as a shield or wall in case the ball is mishandled.
3. For balls difficult to field, the outfielder may assume a position of one knee on the ground in order to block the ball. Blocking the ball is necessary in the following circumstances:
    a. When a single is hit to an outfielder and no one is on base, the fielder must not risk the ball getting by, thus allowing the runner to gain an extra base.
    b. When a passed ball would allow a runner to score, giving the team at bat the lead or the game.

4. Outfielders should receive many ground balls during practice. Hard ground balls hit from a short distance will aid the fielder in learning to judge and react to the ball.
5. To judge the speed or spin of the ball, fielders should watch the ball as it comes from the thrower's hand or leaves the bat.
6. "Playing the ball and not letting the ball play you" requires moving toward the ball in an aggressive manner.

Drills

Chicken. Fielders stand facing each other about fifteen feet apart. Each player attempts to roll the ball between the feet of their partner by using quick, hard throws.

Slide or crossover step. The players are scattered approximately eight feet apart, facing a leader. Each player assumes a "ready position" to permit quick movement. On the commands "rightshort" or "leftshort," the group slides two steps to the right or the left when fielding a ball hit a short distance to the side of a player. Likewise, on the commands "far right" or "far left," the group uses the crossover and three sliding steps to the right or left.

Killers. Two players stand facing each other approximately twenty to twenty-five feet apart. One player tosses ground balls quickly in a mixture of right and left directions to the other player to force the fielder to stretch to field the ball. The players change roles after ten ground balls. The drill is more challenging if the thrower Works with two balls at the same time. This causes the fielder to react more rapidly and provides conditioning for the legs.

Pick-up. Two players face each other. One player throws grounders to the other's right, left, or front. Ideally, players should field the tosses without moving their feet.

Catching ground balls. All players assume a double line formation with partners approximately 30 feet apart. One partner throws bouncing balls to the other partner. Before each grounder is thrown, the fielder assumes a "ready position." In order to insure getting the glove down low, the fielder must touch the ground with the glove before catching the oncoming ball. The player fields the ball as quickly as possible and throws the ball back to the first player. After 20 consecutive grounders, players change roles.

Two-line grounders. Two shuttle lines of four or five players face each other.'The first' player in line number I rolls the ball to the first player in line number 2. Player I then runs past player number 2's left shoulder while advancing to the end of number 2's line. Player number 2 moves forward to meet the ball, fields it and immediately rolls the ball to the next player in line number 1. The drill continues at a rapid pace with everyone moving. Another ball may be added in order to make the drill more challenging.

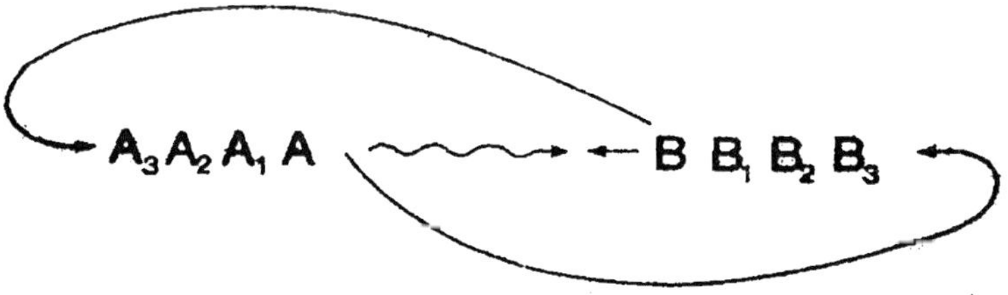

Fig. 1: Two-line grounders

Four-line grounders. All players line up according to the

diagram. The first player in line number I rolls the ball to the first player in line number 2 and goes to the end of that line. The first player in line number 2 fields the ball, rolls it to the first player in fine number 3 and then proceeds to the end of that line. The sequence continues with the first player in the line receiving the ball, then rolling to the first player in the opposite line and going to the end of that line. As the skill level advances, an additional ball may be added.

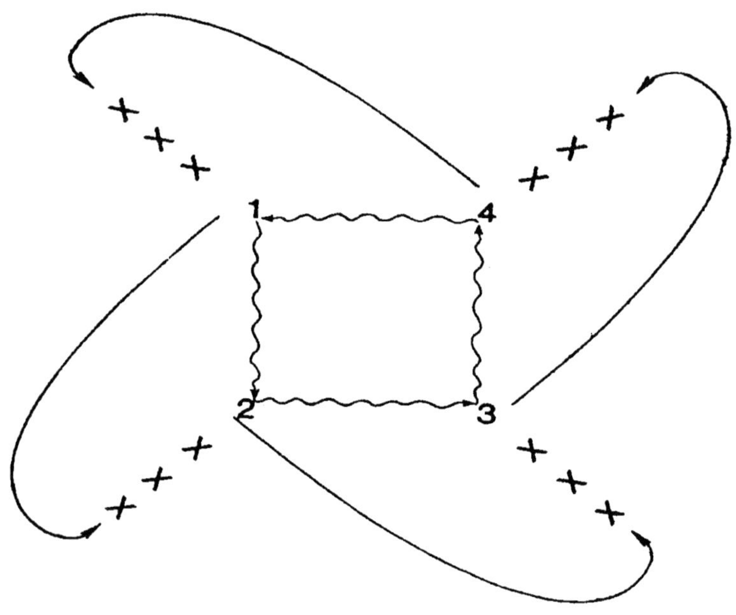

Fig. 2: Four-line grounders

Around the world. Players line tip one behind the other at position number 5. Upon successfully fielding a ground ball, the player moves to position number 4 and so on. Upon committing an error, the player remains at that position until all other players have had their turn. A chance factor may be added. After making an error, a player may chance it to be granted another opportunity at that position. Upon committing a second error, the fielding turn is completed and the player returns to position number 5. The object of the drill is to successfully advance through all positions before the other players.

Shuttle line infield practice. With a fungo hitter, players assume all infield positions except pitching. A series of balls, which include a slow grounder, a hard grounder, and balls to the right and left, are hit alternately to each position. Upon fielding each ball the player throws to first base. After fielding the series of balls, each player rotates clockwise to the next position. This drill may also be used for double play practice.

X
X
X
X
5 4 3 2 1

B

Fig. 3: Around the world

Color throw. Infielders line up in a shuttle line formation at shortstop. Eight balls of four different colors are used for this drill (two yellow, two blue, two green, and two red). The batter randomly selects a ball and hits a grounder to the infielder. The player fields the ball and makes the throw to the appropriate base designated by the color of the ball: yellow, first base; blue, second base; green, third base; red, home.

Fielding hardhit ground balls. Outfielders line up one

behind another, just behind the base path facing the batter. The batter hits a hard ground ball to the first person in the line, who properly fields the ball, throws it to the catcher, and retreats to the end of the line. Ground balls should be hit alternately to the right, left, and directly to the fielder.

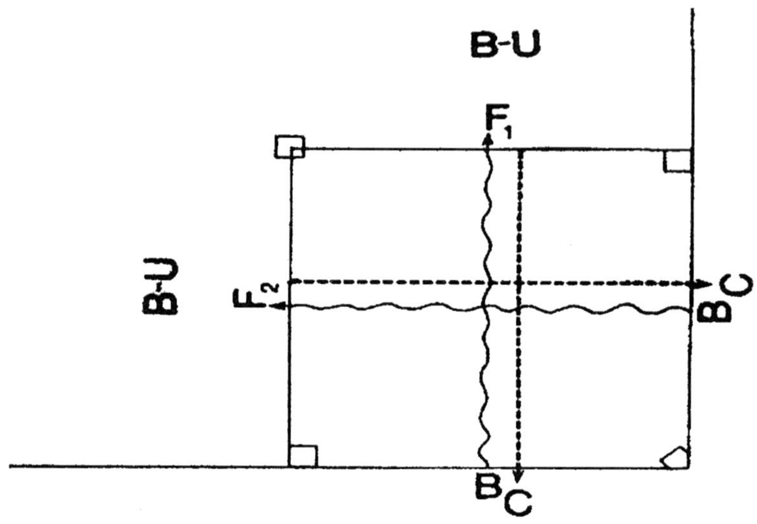

Fig. 4: Continuous catches *Fig. 4: One-ball box drill*

Continuous catches: Fielder number I takes a position halfway between first and second base behind the base path. Fielder number 2 takes a similar position halfway between second and third. Backup fielders are positioned behind fielders number I and 2. A batter and catcher take a position opposite each fielder, and the batter fungo hits ground balls to the fielder. Fielders return the balls to their respective catchers. The batter continues hitting to the fielder until an error is made. As skill improves, the ground balls should be hit so they are more difficult to field.

One-ball box drill: Sixteen players are involved in this drill: four batters, four catchers, four fielders, and four backup players. The batters are placed along the foul lines between home and third, and home and first; two to each side. Each batter has a catcher. Batters along the first base line hit grounders to the shortstop and the third basernan. Respectively, batters on the third base line hit grounders to the first and second basemen, Each fielder fields the ball and returns it to the batter's catcher. Backup players retrieve balls missed by fielders. Players rotate within groups on a signal. To avoid being hit by another ball, fielders should not cross the base line to field the ball. Option: Initially, fielders may roll the ball back to the catcher.

Two-ball box drill. This drill is the same as the one-ball box drill except the batter hits a second ball as the fielder throws the first ball to the catcher. All players must remain alert in this drill.

Fielding fly balls

Often beginners need special help and practice when learning to judge, and get into position for, easy pop-fly balls and balls hit in front, behind, and to the right and left of the body.

Performance description

I. Assume a ready position with the hips and knees bent, the feet spread and the weight evenly distributed on the balls of the feet.

2. Move to a position in line with and under the ball as soon as the ball is hit.

3. Use a crossover step when moving to field balls to the right or left of the body. When retreating in a

backward right direction, pivot on the right foot, view the ball over the left shoulder and run diagonally to a position for the catch.

4. Watch the ball.
5. Position the non-throwing side foot forward,
6. Attempt to catch the ball approximately shoulder high on the throwing side of the body.
7. Catch with two hands.
8. Prepare for the throw.

Common errors

1. Failure to be alert, thus getting a late start on the ball.
2. Failure to adequately judge the ball, resulting in overrunning and allowing the ball to drop to the ground.
3. Preparing to throw before actually catching the ball.
4. Closing the glove too soon.
5. Improper glove position.

Teaching tips and strategy

1. Experience is the best method of learning to judge the flight of the ball and of moving into the proper position. Players frequently have difficulty judging the flight of line drives and "texas leaguers."
2. Players should run smoothly to the ball. A flatfooted run hinders judging the ball as it jars the eyes, head, and body.
3. Sunglasses or the glove may be used to shield the eyes from the sun.

4. Players should "call" for the ball in order to avoid confusion and collisions. Call out "mine," because the phrases "I've got it" or "III take it" may be confused with "You've got it" or "you take it." Generally, the first player to call for the ball should attempt the catch and the other player acknowledges by calling the fielder's name and moving bchind the fielder.
5. When the ball is hit between outfielders, the player who can receive the ball on the glove side of the body calls for the ball and attempts the catch. The other player assumes a back up position.
6. Fielders should not be permitted to take more than one or two steps back peddling for deeply hit balls.
7. Generally, balls hit midway between the infield and outfield should be played by the outfielder as it is easier to run forward than backward and the forward momentum aids the throw after the catch. The outfielder should decide and signal who will make the catch.
8. Fielders should practice fielding pitched balls as well as balls that have been fungo Wt.

Drills

Pop-fly drill. Infielders assume their normal positions. The batter fungo-hits pop flies near the pitcher's plate and home plate, offering the pitcher, catcher, and infielders opportunities for play. Each fielder calls for the ball prior to catching it.

Chasing fly balls. Fielders line up one behind another in left field. On signal, the first player runs at top speed toward center field. The coach throws or hits a ball which leads the fielder. After catching the ball, the fielder throws to the catcher and remains in center field until all players have moved in that direction. Fielders then practice chasing balls while moving toward left field. The coach continues to throw or hit balls until each player has made ten trips (five in each direction).

Changing directions. Players assume a scattered formation facing the leader. On the leader's command, players will run forward or backward, slide right or left, or turn and run backward-right or backward-left.

Sensational catches. The fielders line up in center field one behind the other and await their turns. A ball is thrown in front of, behind, to the right of, or to the left of each fielder at a distance that will force the fielder to catch the ball while running at top speed. The ball is quickly returned to the thrower.

Hits between infielders and outfielders. The batter hits short fly balls into areas between the infielders and outfielders. Players practice calling for each ball and outfielders will back the infielders in front of them. Outfielders must practice calling off infielders while moving toward the ball to make the catch.

Backing up

Performance description

1. Get in line with the ball and assume a position of seven to ten feet behind the player fielding the ball.

2. Avoid distracting the fielder.

3. Be prepared to catch any deflected balls or balls getting by the fielder.

Common errors

1. Interfering with the fielder catching the ball.
2. Not hustling into backup position as soon as the ball is hit.

Teaching tips and strategy

I. The outfielders have a responsibility to backup on every play.

2. The left fielder backs up:
   a. The center fielder on balls hit to left-center field.
   b. Second base on throws from first and from the right fielder.
   c. The third baseman on balls hit to that position, rundowns or throws from the catcher, pitcher, first and second basemen, and the right and center fielders.
   d. The shortstop on all balls hit in that direction.
3. The center fielder backs up:
   a. The left and right fielder.
   b. Second base or balls hit to that position, rundowns and on throws from the catcher, pitcher, first and third basemen.
   c. The shortstop on all balls hit to that position,
4. The right fielder backs up:
   a. The center fielder on all balls hit to right-center field.
   b. First base on all balls hit or thrown to that position.

   c. Second base on throws from the third baseman, shortstop and left fielder and rundowns between second and third bases.

5. The shortstop backs up second and third bases on attempted steals and throws from the outfield, and the third baseman when fielding batted balls.
6. The second baseman's responsibilities include backing up second base when the shortstop is taking throws from the left fielder, pitcher, catcher, and the first baseman.
7. When a runner is not in scoring position, the catcher backs up first base.
8. The pitcher backs up throws to home and third base when runners are on base.

Covering

Performance description

1. Know the responsibilities for covering a base in the various situations.
2. Move quickly to a position with one foot on the side of the base nearest the player fielding the ball.
3. Prepare to take the throw and execute the necessary play.

Teaching tips and strategy

1. The shortstop is responsible for covering second base when the ball is hit to the right of the field, and a play at second or a double play will be attempted. The shortstop also covers second on a double play attempt fielded by the first baseman. In this case the shortstop tags second base and relays the ball to first base covered by the second

baseman. Third base must be covered when a runner is advancing to that base, and the third baseman is pulled away from the base to field a ball.

2. When the first baseman is pulled off the bag, the base may be covered by the pitcher or second baseman depending on the play. The shortstop covers second if the second baseman moves to first. On double play attempts when the ball is hit to the left side of the field, the second baseman covers second and relays the ball to first.

3. On overthrows or passed balls at home, the pitcher covers home plate.

Double play

Performance description

I. The basics of the double play involving the shortstop and second baseman consist of the following: a. The player fielding the ball must know the speed and ability of the pivot person and time the throw so it reaches the bag at the same time as the pivot person.

2. The pivot person should:
   a. Approach the base on a straight line with the throw.
   b. Make a target with the glove about chin high.
   c. Catch the ball with both hands as the bag is contacted with the non-throwing side foot.
   d. Take another step after tagging the base, pivot on the throwing foot, and step toward first base.
   e. Make the throw quickly and accurately with a snap or sidearm throw.

f. Get off the bag quickly to avoid collision with the advancing runner.

Common errors

1. Improper timing in receiving the throw.
2. Not leaving the base after catching the ball in order to avoid an advancing baserunner.

Teaching tips and strategy

1. The pivot player should:
   a. Hustle to the base to receive the throw on arrival, as it is better to be early than late. The approach to the base should be in line with the oncoming throw and the bag.
   b. Do not throw to the next base if a play is not possible.
   c. Always be ready for a poor throw from the fielder.
   d. Be sure the foot is in contact with the bag when the ball is in the glove.
2. When the ball is fielded close to a base, the fielder should touch the base unassisted, and relay the throw.

Drills

Keystone combo. The coach alternates hitting ground balls to the second baseman and to the shortstop. The fielders take turns fielding, covering the bag, and throwing to first. Double play practice. Batter is equipped with five or six balls.

1. A ground ball is fungo hit to the third baseman who throws to the second baseman who is covering

second. The second baseman then relays the ball to first base.

2. A grounder is fungo hit to the shortstop, who throws to the second baseman covering the base. The second baseman then makes the relay to first.
3. The batter repeats the action to the right side of the infield, starting with the second baseman who throws to the shortstop covering second, and relays the ball to first.
4. A short ball is fungo hit in front of the plate to be fielded by the catcher, thrown to second, and relayed to first.

Turning two. The batter fungo hits grounders to various infielders. A player representing the batter runs to first base. Simultaneously a base runner on first attempts to reach second. Infielders attempt to successfully complete a double play.

Relay

The relay is a method of getting the ball from a deep outfield position to the infield by using two or three throws instead of one long throw. This technique offers the relayer options as to where to attempt a putout. On the other hand, if the ball is thrown a long distance from left field to home or third, the team forfeits its opportunity to make a play at another base. The relay is also a valuable tool when the outfielders lack the accuracy or strength to effectively throw the ball a long distance.

Performance description

1. Go to a position slightly beyond the infield toward the outfielder fielding the ball.

2. Get in a direct line between the outfielder and the base to which the throw is to be made.
3. Wave the arms to signal to the outfielder the direction of the throw.
4. Make a target with the glove on the non-throwing side.
5. Attempt to catch the ball on the non throwing side, pivot and throw.

Common errors

1. Failure to use the relay.
2. Not getting in direct line between the outfielder and the intended base.

Teaching tips and strategy

1. Depending on the situation, the first baseman, second baseman, or shortstop, acts as the relay player.
2. If the second baseman serves as the relay person, the shortstop verbally signals where the relayer should throw the ball and vice versa. Depending on the situation, verbal signals such as "third," "second," or "no play," should be given. Valuable time may be gained if the relay player knows where to throw the ball before catching it.

Drills

Outfield relay. Players line up according to the diagram following. The batter hits fly balls to the fielder. The fielder catches the ball and throws it to the relay player, who has moved into the proper position. The ball is then relayed to the catcher.

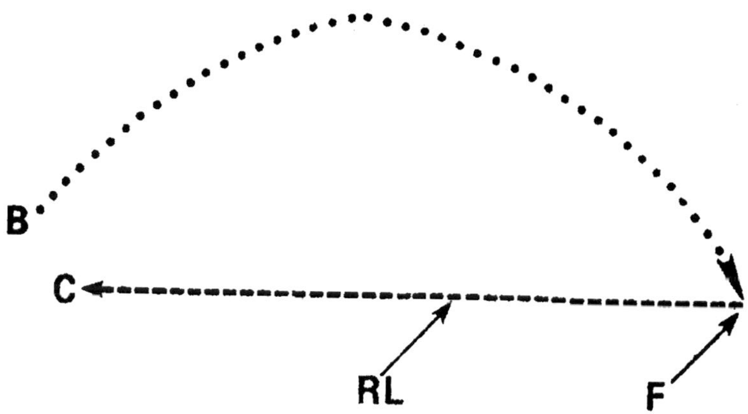

Fig. : Outfield relay

Deep hits and relay. Batter fungo hits deep fly balls to the outfielders who are stationed in normal positions. The shortstop goes into the outfield to relay all throws returned from left and left-center field. The second baseman acts as the relay for balls thrown from right and right-center field. The player not receiving the relay (second baseman or shortstop) should give the relay player directions as to where to throw the ball in the infield.

Putting out a runner

Performance description

I. If the runner is sliding into the base, assume a position straddling the base, and watch the ball until it is in the glove. Catch the ball with both hands, and lay the back of the gloved hand between the base and the runner's path. After making the tag immediately move from the base.

2. In a force out, tag the base, and move immediately from the base.

3. When the tag is made off of the base, tag the runner with the ball in the glove.

Common errors

1. Blocking the base without having possession of the ball.
2. Watching the approaching runner rather than the ball.
3. Failure to get out of the way after making the tag.

Teaching tips and strategy

1. Mishandled balls should be picked up with both hands. The eyes should be focused on the ball, not the runner.
2. Before each pitch the fielder should know the number of balls and strikes, the score, the position of the runners, and where the play should be made.

Drills

Tag out. The second baseman and shortstop assume normal positions with a runner halfway between first and second. The second baseman covering the base receives the throw from the catcher. The appropriate tag is made.

Force out. The second baseman and shortstop assume normal positions with a runner on first. The ball is hit to the second baseman who tosses to the shortstop who quickly moves off the base.

Tips on paying defensive positions

First baseman

Attributes

I. A tall player, with good body extension, presents a target for the fielders making a throw.

2. A left-handed first baseman has an advantage in fielding bunts and throwing to other bases.
3. The first baseman must be able to catch high and low throws with one hand as well as two.

Responsibilities

1. The first baseman is responsible for covering the base on all plays and pickoff attempts at first, fielding bunts down the first base line, and relaying the ball from right field.

Techniques and strategies

1. In fast pitch with no one on the base, the first baseman should play approximately five to six feet from the foul line and four to five feet in front of the baseline. For the same situation in slow pitch, the baseman should be approximately eight to ten feet behind the baseline and eight feet toward second base.
2. In fast pitch with two strikes on the batter and the threat of bunting reduced, the first baseman should move to a position behind the baseline.
3. In fast pitch with a runner on first base, the baseman should assume a position approximately fifteen feet in front of the base, when anticipating a bunt.
4. As the ball is hit, the baseman should turn and move quickly to the base, face the thrower, and extend the glove or mitt forward about shoulder high as a target.
5. When stretching toward the throw, the foot on the glove or mitt side should be extended as far as

possible toward the ball. The other foot tags the inside of the bag and is quickly removed after the catch to avoid the runner.

6. On a pickoff attempt, the baseman should straddle the bag and make the glove tag low by the inside of the base.

7. For faulty throws it may be necessary to leave the base to make the catch. Once the ball is caught, the runner may be tagged.

Second baseman

Attributes

1. The second baseman must be quick, agile, and adept at throwing from off-balanced positions after catching a ball.

Responsibilities

The second baseman is responsible for covering the bag and Pickoffs, and Plays at second base on balls hit to the left side of field. In addition, the baseman may act as a relay for deep balls from right and center field.

Techniques and strategies

1. The baseman's position is approximately 15 feet off the base and ten feet behind the baseline. This position varies according to the player's lateral fielding ability and if a runner is on first base hin In the latter case, the baseman moves cloer to second base.

2. When covering the base on close plays, the baseman should stretch toward the oncoming ball.

3. In covering second base on the forced double play, the baseman touches the bag with the right toot,

steps to the inside of the base arid pivots on the left foot to execute the relay to first.

4. With a runner on first, and a ground ball hit to the second baseman, a tag on the runner and a throw to first base should be the preferable play. If the runner attempts to avoid the tag by slowing down or running wide, the throw sho uld be inade to the shortstop covering second base. the throw should be made to the shortstop covering second base.

Shortstop

Attributes

1. The shortstop maybe considered the key player in the infield due to tile involvement innumerous Plays and being in a Position to direct play.
2. The position requires speed a strong and accurate arm, and good lateral coverage.
3. The ability to charge balls, throw sidearm, cover second, relay ball from deep left field, and back up second and third bases instinctively a necessary attributes for the position.

Responsibilities

1. Cover second base on the double play when the throw is coming from the right side of the field.
2. Backing up the second baseman to throws to second from the catcher, pitcher, first baseman, right or center field.
3. Act as relay from left field.
4. Cover third base on hunted balls.
5. Back up third on fly balls to the outfield.

Techniques and strategies

1. With no one on base, the shortstop assumes a position 20-25 feet from second base and 10 feet behind the baseline. With runners on base, the player may move in approximately four feet and slightly toward second.
2. In a double play situation, on balls hit to the shortstop's left and close to the bag, the player may make the play unassisted by touching second and relaying to first. If the shortstop is moving in a line other than toward second base when fielding, an underhand or snap throw may be appropriate.
3. When covering the initial base on a double play, the shortstop should catch the throw as the left foot touches the bag, step off the bag with the right foot and throw while stepping onto the left foot.

Third baseman

Attributes

1. Playing the "hot corner" effectively requires courage, quick reactions, sure hands and a strong, accurate arm.

Responsibilities

1. The third baseman's responsibilities include fielding bunted balls down the baseline, catching shallow pop-ups in fair or foul territory, covering third base on steals, force plays, and pickoffs.

Techniques and strategies

With no one on base, the third baseman plays three to four feet from the foul line and approximately even with or slightly behind the base.

2. With a runner on first and less than two outs, the baseman assumes a position three to four feet closer to home plate.
3. On slow hit balls toward shortstop, the baseman should move diagonally toward first and field the ball.
4. The third baseman may be in a better position than the pitcher and catcher for fielding a bunt down the third base line.
5. Proper positioning for a tag play includes straddling the base with the glove low. For a force out the base is touched with either foot and a step out of the base path is taken.

Catcher

Attributes

1. The catcher should possess leadership abilities and be able to work closely with the pitcher in determining the pitches to be thrown.
2. An agile and flexible catcher has an advantage in being able to come from a squatting to a throwing position quickly.
3. The catcher should develop a good overhand throw because of its strength and accuracy and it eliminates the possibility of hitting left-handed batters with the throw.
4. In fast pitch, a catcher with a strong arm and quick release discourages runners from stealing.
5. The catcher should be physically strong and able to out runners charging home plate.

6. The catcher should be able to concentrate on catching the ball and not be distracted by the batter or baserunner.

Responsibilities

1. Making a signal for the pitcher.
2. Covering home plate.
3. Backing up first and third base.
4. Preventing a steal.
5. Fielding bunts and pop-ups around home plate.

Techniques and strategies

1. The catcher squats with the weight evenly distributed on both feet which may be in a parallel or slightly forward stride position.
2. In fast pitch, a target is made with the mitt at shoulder height; in slow pitch the mitt is held on or near the ground slightly in front of the catcher.
3. The throwing hand should be protected by making a fist and placing it to the side of and in back of the mitt or glove.
4. When anticipating a steal, the catcher should go into a semi-squat position rather than a full squat.
5. Throws to a base should be made only when a putout is possible.
6. On a steal play with runners on first and third, hold the runner on third before attempting a throw to second.
7. When tagging a runner at home plate, assume a forward stride position in front of the plate facing

the throw, catch the ball and turn toward the runner placing the glove low and in the base path so the runner's lead foot cannot touch the plate without being tagged.

Outfield

Attributes

1. Outfielders should have strong throwing arms, speed, and the ability to judge and catch fly balls.

Responsibilities

1. The responsibilities of an outfielder include backing up appropriate infielders, adjacent outfielders, and plays at the closest bases. Catching all balls within reach requires the outfielder to be alert and moving on every play.

2. In fast pitch, the center fielder is the key outfielder with responsibility for covering the largest territory and backing up both adjacent fielders. In slow pitch, the center fielder's responsibilities are shared by the short or roving fielder.

Techniques and strategies

1. On sharply hit balls to short Tight field with no one on base, or possibly a runner on first, the fielder may attempt a putout at first. Other fielders should throw to second base.

2. With one of the runners on third, after catching a fly ball the throw should be made to home plate. A fielded ground ball should be thrown into second or third.

3. On a long foul ball a runner on third may tag up and advance home after the catch. Therefore, the

fielder should be in a position to make a throw to home plate.

4. Throws to home or third base should be kept low to save time, to allow a possible cutoff, and to assist the baseman in making the tag on a runner.

5. For each new batter, the outfielder assumes 4, position according to the ability of the batter and the game situation. This player must anticipate either a fly ball, grounder or line drive and know the appropriate action for cacti.

6. On balls hit between fielders, one should call for the ball and attempt to cut the ball off while the other assumes a backup position.

7. As one fielder retrieves a deeply hit passed ball, the adjacent fielder assumes a relay position.

8. In slow pitch softball, a tenth player is designated as the short fielder or "roving fielder." The short fielder's position is between the infielders and outfielders, either to the right or left of second base depending on the strategy chosen for a particular batter. As a rover, the player assumes an outfielder's position in left-center or right-center field at a depth equal to the other outfielders. This formation is commonly referred to as "the fan" or the "umbrella."

Offensive skills: Batting

Being a successful batter involves more than simply hitting the ball. Players who understand the strategy of batting and who can capitalize on personal Strengths will be a valuable asset to a team. In addition to being able to hit the ball with power and accuracy, a good batter must also be able to study the pitcher, know when to take pitches, when to try for a walk, and which pitch to hit.

Performance description

1. Grip the bat with the dominant hand above and adjacent to the non-dominant hand. Align the second joints of the top hand midway between the knuckles and second joints of the bottom hand.
2. Stand with the feet comfortably apart and the front of the body facing the plate. Bend the knees and evenly distribute the weight.
3. Turn the head to look at the pitcher.
4. Bring the hands and bat to a position approximately shoulder high and slightly behind the back foot. The non-dominant arm is extended across the body and is held nearly parallel to the ground. The elbow of the dominant arm is bent and held away from the body. Cock the wrists and hold the bat in an upright or angular position. Watch the ball until it makes contact with the bat.
5. Begin the swing by striding toward the ball with the front foot. Sequentially rotate the hips, trunk, and shoulder toward the pitcher. Extend the arms, snap the wrists and contact the ball in front of front hip.
6. Follow through and drop the bat.

Common errors

I. Separating the hands on the grip.
2. Assuming a stance in which the front of the body is turned toward the pitcher.

3. Holding the rear elbow close to the body.
4. Closing the eyes or lifting the head just prior to the hit.
5. Failure to transfer the weight.
6. Failure to follow through.
7. Swinging too early or too late.

Teaching tips and strategy

1. Players with poor eye-hand coordination often profit from hitting the ban from a batting tee. The batting tee allows the beginner to develop a complete, level swing without involving the problem of contacting a moving ball. In addition, it can be used to develop the basic swing. Emphasis should be placed on watching the ball and keeping the head down and stable throughout the swing. The tee should be positioned so the ball is contacted just in front of the forward hip.
2. The standard grip or "choke" grip is recommended for beginners.
3. Whether hitting a teed or pitched ball, choking up on the bat helps many batters have better control, thus they are more successful in making contact with the ball. The teacher should stress that the batter keep the butt end of the bat level during the swing. This helps to eliminate the problem of bruising the arms or stomach by hitting them with the butt of the bat. Frequently, this difficulty results from poor technique, using a bat that is too heavy, or both.

If players consistently hit grounders or pop-ups they

should be reminded to execute a level follow through. Once the forward motion of the bat has begun, the hands should remain on a level plane below the shoulder.

Players should be taught to use a bat they can comfortably swing and keep under control. The first consideration in hitting should be controlling the bat and contacting the ball solidly. After control is achieved, the player should strive for power. Beginning players often have difficulty in hitting a pitched ball because of their eagerness to hit the ball hard. Drills should be used which will alleviate this problem and emphasize bat control.

6. Players often lift their heads before contact is made with the ball. Having the batter look for the seams or look for the color of a dot painted on the ball aids the player in watching the ball more effectively.

7. To correct an incomplete follow through, some teachers and coaches have found it helpful to place a towel or make a target area behind the batter's foot nearest the pitcher. The batter should complete the follow-through and drop the bat on the target. This habit also helps insure that the bat is not thrown in a dangerous manner.

8. Players should be instructed when to "hit away" or "take a pitch." For example, with three balls and one strike, the batter should hit the next pitch if it is in the strike zone. However, if the count is three balls and no strikes, the batter should not attempt to hit the next pitch. This situation forces the pitcher to throw a strike or relinquish a walk.

Drills

Batting tee. With fielders in normal positions the ball is placed on a batting tee. The batter then hits the stationary ball into the field. The batter is allowed a designated number of hits, then replaces a teammate in the field to allow each player to have a turn at bat. Emphasis should be placed on a level swing of the bat, keeping the eye on the ball, coordinating the swing with the shift in weight, and swinging through the ball. Another alternative is to use the batting tee while playing many of the suggested lead-up games.

Pepper. Four to six players line up side by side facing a batter 20 feet away. The fielders pitch balls to the batter who hits grounders back to the fielders. Momentum may be added to the drill by using two balls.

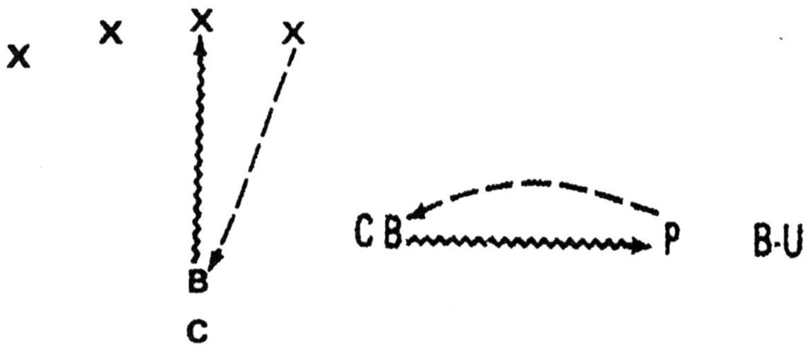

Fig. : Pepper

Fig. : Four-player pepper

Four-player pepper. Players line up according to the diagram. The pitcher tosses to the batter. The batter hits the ball back to the pitcher. A backup player retrieves balls missed by the pitcher. A catcher retrieves balls missed by the batter. Positions are rotated after ten or 15 hits.

Hit and run. Each batter attempts to hit a designated number of pitched balls. On the final hit, the batter runs to first base at top speed.

Fungo hitting. Outfielders assume normal defensive positions. A batter fungo hits to alternate fields for place-hitting practice. Fielders return balls to the catcher. After ten successive hits all players rotate positions clockwise.

Line ball. With six on a team, players face each other in two parallel lines 60 feet apart. Each team or side has a bat. A player on one team fungo hits a ground ball, attempting to drive the grounder through the other team's line of fielders. Team "B" likewise tries to bat the ball across the opponent's fine. The bat is passed down the line so each player has an opportunity. As a safety precaution, be sure there is sufficient space between the players in the lines, only one team bats at a time, and the players call for the ball when fielding it.

Baserunning

Baserunning skills should not be overlooked in the early stages of overall skill development. Whether the game is won or lost is often determined by a team's baserunning skill and strategy.

Running from the Batter's Box

Performance description

1. After hitting the ball and dropping the bat, step toward first base with the rear foot.
2, Advance toward first with the head up and the eyes focusing down the base path. Swing the, arms freely, and push off with the balls of the feet.

3. On short pop-ups or any balls playable at first, run beyond first base at full speed.
4. If it is determined that an attempt should be made to continue to second base, swing outward five to six feet to the right of the base line approximately 15 feet before first base. This manuever provides the best angle for continuing to second. Touch first base as the turn is made toward second.

Common errors

1. Waiting to see if the ball is caught before running to first base.
2. Missing the base.
3. Stopping at first base rather than crossing it or rounding the bag.

Performance description

1. While waiting for the pitch, face the next base.
2. Place the left foot in a push-off position on the inside of the base.
3. Point the right foot toward the next base and shift the body weight forward.
4. Allow the arms to hang freely.
5. Flex the knees and bend the torso forward,
6. Begin the run by pushing off with the back foot.

Common errors

1. Watching the ball rather than focusing on the base.
2. Hesitating before sprinting.
3. Failure to listen to or watch for the base coach's signal.

4. Improperly rounding the base, resulting in a wide turn.
5. Missing the base.

Teaching tips and strategy

1. In slow-pitch the baserunner should leave the base when the ball crosses home plate or is hit. Fast pitch rules permit baserunners to lead off as the ball leaves the pitcher's hand.
2. Baserunners should attempt to take as many bases as possible on each hit without being overly risky.
3. With two outs all, baserunners should advance as soon as the ball is hit.
4. When on third base with less than two outs, the runner should return to or stay on the base when fly balls are hit to the outfield. As the ball is caught, the coach signals the runner to sprint home.
5. A batterbaserunner advancing from home to first or from third to home should run in foul territory to avoid being hit by a batted or thrown ball.
6. Baserunners should run behind a player fielding a ball in the baseline to avoid interference or being tagged.
7. When a player is on second or third base and the ball is hit to an infielder, the runner should take a short leadoff and wait until the fielder throws to first before advancing.
8. The outward curve previously described for rounding first base is applied to each subsequent base when more than one base is attempted. The inside comer of the base may be touched with

either foot as the runner pivots toward the next base.

9. Upon approaching second, the baserunner looks to the third base coach for directions to take the turn or to stop at the base. The third base coach will also signal directions to runners approaching third,

10. To practice running beyond first base, draw a line 20 feet beyond the base, perpendicular to the baseline.

Drills

Take off. The baserunner starts at home plate. After a mock swing, the runner takes five to six powerful strides out of the batter's box with eyes focused on the first base coach. The player jogs the remaining distance to first base. As the runner rounds the base, five to six powerful strides toward second are taken, The runner continues this procedure at every base.

Base cornering. Players line up single file behind home plate. The first player runs at top speed to first base and makes a turn as if going to second. After making the turn, the player jogs back to home plate. One at a time each player repeats this action.

Sprints. Starting at home plate, the player runs three continuous sprints around the bases. After resting five seconds, two sprints are run. The player rests another five seconds and runs one final sprint.

Rabbit. Eight runners are placed as shown in the diagram. On the signal "go" all players run and attempt to tag the player preceding them. Upon making a tag, the player who committed the tag may leave the drill. The tagged player must continue until tagging the preceding runner or the drill is discontinued.

Designated situations

The following game-like situations provide excellent practice for competition.

1. The batter hits a pitched ball to the infield and runs to first base. A baserunner may be placed beside the batter for the actual running.
2. The batter fungo hits a single to left field. The batter/ baserunner touches first base and makes a turn toward second. If the ball is not fielded cleanly, the runner then advances to second.
3. With a runner on first, the batter fungo hits a single. The advancing baserunner looks at the third base coach just before touching second base, and either stops or continues as signaled.
4. With a runner on second base, a batter fungo hits a base hit. The runner on second attempts to score.
5. With a runner on second, the batter fungo hits a ball in front of the runner to the shortstop. The runner takes a lead, then advances as the throw is made to first base.
6. With a runner on second, a batter hits between the first and second baseman. The runner attempts to advance to third.

Sacrifice fly

With less than two outs, a sacrifice fly may be used to advance a baserunner at the expense of the batter being put out. This technique is frequently used to score a runner or place a runner in scoring position.

Performance description

1. The batter hits a long fly ball to the outfield,
2. The baserunner stays on the base in the takeoff position,
3. As the ball is caught or missed the baserunner sprints to the next base.

Common errors

1. Inability of the batter to hit the ball to the outfield.
2. Failure of the baserunner to tag the base and leave immediately when the ball is caught,
3. Leaving the base before the ball is caught forcing a retreat to tag up before an advance is possible.
4. Failure of the baserunner to listen to the base coach.

Drills

1. The batter hits a long fly ball to the outfield, the baserunner "tags up" at the base. As the ball is caught or missed the baserunner runs to the next base.

Teaching tips

1. When there are less than two outs, a sacrifice fly may be used to advance a baserunner at the expense of the batter being put out.
2. Often the baserunner will cause the fielder to hurry and make a throwing error by faking an advance for the next base. If an error is made and the situation warrants, the baserunner advances.

5

TEACHING ADVANCED SKILLS

In advanced level play, a player must possess the ability to think quickly, charge the ball, throw on the run, bunt, and place hit. Although new skills are introduced at this level, continuing emphasis should be placed on developing existing skills.

Mastery of the techniques and activities in this chapter should be a challenge to the advanced player. Quickness, accuracy, and excellence in every aspect of the game should be a meaningful theme for all practices. Furthermore, many of the suggested drills are designed to promote player concentration and preparedness through performance of skills in game-like situations.

Advanced throwing and catching

Advanced players must be able to catch hardhit or thrown balls safely and without error. In improving their throwing techniques, players should strive for quick releases and accuracy. Hustling tactics, including charging shallow balls and throwing on the run, should be a part of each player's skill repertoire. Through challenging practices, which place increasing demands on the players, basic skills may be further developed. At this level, each player should be encouraged to increase personal expectations and develop self-motivation for improvement.

Performance description

1. Emphasize "giving" with the ball when catching hard throws or batted balls by relaxing and recoiling arms.
2. Quickly move to fielding position, in line with the ball, as soon as the ball is hit or thrown.
3. On quick release throws, snap the wrist, shift weight forward, and follow through.
4. For throwing on the run, position body in line with intended throw, then field and throw without breaking stride.

Common errors

1. Overrunning the ball when charging grounders,
2. Failure to watch the ball into the glove when preparing for a quick throw.

Teaching tips and strategy

1. For fielding and throwing on the run, good timing and a strong arm and wrist must be developed.

Drill

Burn out. Two players face each other approximately 30 feet apart. Using one ban, players throw back and forth as quickly and as hard as possible.

Double bell warm-up. Two players, each with a ball, face one another. Using, an overhand throw, players simultaneously throw the ball back and forth.

Bullet. Several runners line up on the first baseline approximately five feet from home plate. The infielders assume their normal positions. The coach hits a firm grounder to any fielder. The fielder charges the ball, fields it, and throws to first base in one motion. The runner attempts to beat the throw to first base.

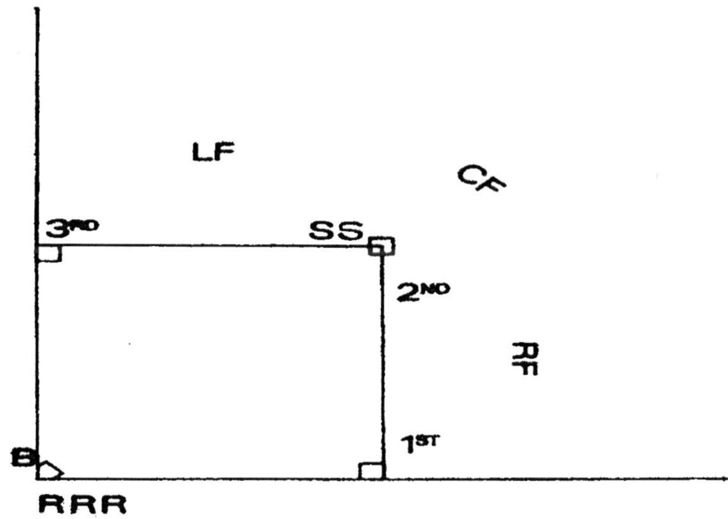

Fig. 1: Bullet

The sidearm throw

Infielders must be able to field balls with a quick release on the throw. The side arm throw enables the quickest release and should be executed for moderate distances, without sacrificing accuracy.

Performance description

1. Turn the torso so the non-throwing side faces the target.
2. Extend the upper arm diagonally out and down from the shoulder while extending the forearm directly up from the elbow.

3. Drop the forearm to a position parallel with the ground as the arm moves forward.
4. Transfer weight to the forward foot and rotate the torso toward the target.
5. As arm moves forward, release the ball with a wrist snap and follow through across the body.

Common errors

1. Tenseness in the throw.
2. Failure to transfer the weight and snap the wrist to give force to the throw.

Teaching tips and strategy

1. Players must have full control of the ball prior to executing the throw.
2. If time does not permit throwing from an upright position, the throw may be made with the trunk bent and the arm moving in a horizontal plane below shoulder level.
3. Fielding the ball with the throwing hand should be attempted only if the ball is stopped or moving slowly, and time does not permit proper fielding.

Drills

Infield throwing and catching. The coach or player rolls a ball directly to an infielder in normal position. The infielder fields the ball and throws sidearm to a designated base. The ball is then rolled to the side of the infielder, who uses a crossover step to move into position to field the ball and throws to a designated base. Another ball is then rolled directly to the infielder, who from a low position makes a quick sidearm throw to the designated base.

Barehand. The infielders take their respective positions. The coach rolls the ban to each infielder in turn. Each player fields the ball barehanded and throws to first. Emphasis should be placed on fielding and throwing in the same motion.

Fast-pitch pitching

Advanced pitching in fast-pitch softball involves controlling the speed, spin, and placement of the ball. The development of an accurate, straight, fastball is basic to a softball pitcher. Once this pitch is mastered, curved bails and various windups add versatility and keep batters uncertain regarding expected pitches.

Fastball

Performance description

1. Use a tripod grip or the five-fingered grip, if the hand is small.
2. With the ball in front of the body, take a position with both feet in contact with the pitcher's plate.
3. As the backswing is taken, keep the pivot foot in contact with the pitcher's plate, and rotate the trunk slightly away from home plate.
4. Swing the arm back in a pendular motion and forward, extending the elbow and facing the batter on the downswing. Step forward with the opposite foot as the downswing begins.
5. As the ball begins to roll off the fingers below hip level, snap the wrist upward.
6. Follow through with the elbow straight.
7. Assume ready fielding position off the plate.

Common errors

1. Holding the ball in the palm.
2. Releasing the ball late, resulting in a high pitch.
3. Releasing the ball early resulting in a low pitch.
4. Following through in an off-balanced position.
5. Failure to swing the arm parallel to the body and straight through on the release.

Curveball

Performance description

I. Grip the ball with the fingers on the outside of the ball.

2. Use footwork as in fastball.
3. On releasing the ball, rotate the arm and hand inward causing the ball to curve right to left, or left to right for left-handed pitchers.
4. Follow through straight ahead with palm facing downward.
5. For an incurve pitch, the arm is rotated outward instead of inward.

Windups

Performance description

I. *Windmill.* Make a full circle by swinging the arm forward, upward, around, and through by the hip. Twist the body slightly away from the batter and initiate forward step as the ball is raised. Do not lock the elbow until the forward swing begins. Whip arm down and through as the body quickly twists towards the batter. Release the ball with a wrist snap and follow through.

2. Half windmill. Bring the ball back, with a bent arm, approximately head high and rotate the body away from home plate. On the forward step, swing the arm downward and through, turning the body back toward home. Snap the wrist on the release.

Pitcher-vs-pitcher. Two pitchers work as a battery. One player pitches balls to the other who acts as the catcher. The "catcher" calls balls and strikes, with imaginary batters registering strike outs or walks. Any "batter" who receives a walk becomes a "baserunner," and progresses with subsequent walks. After three outs, the pitcher and catcher switch positions to finish the inning. Players compete for the fewest runs in a set number of innings.

Infield

Advanced players must develop their existing skills in lateral fielding, charging ground balls, throwing on the run, backing up, relaying and covering. In addition, infielders must be familiar with their responsibilities in executing rundowns, cutoffs, and fielding hunted balls in order to maximize defensive team play and avoid confusion when these situations arise.

Rundown

The rundown is used when a baserunner is trapped between two bases. Team effort is necessary as the defensive players close in on the runner from both sides.

Performance description

1. The first and second basemen assume positions close to their respective bases. The hall is thrown to the second baseman.

2. The catcher and shortstop back up the basemen.
3. The second baseman forces the runner back toward first base by holding the hall in a throwing position and charging the runner.
4. The shortstop assumes a position on second base.
5. The second baseman throws to first baseman to tag the runner and retreats to back up the shortstop if the tag is unsuccessful.
6. If the runner changes direction and moves toward second base, the first baseman charges the runner and throws to the shortstop for the tag.
7. If the tag is not successful, the catcher assumes a position on first. The first baseman retreats to back up catcher.

Common errors

1. Allowing too many throws before attempting the tag.
2. Failure to have runners on other bases under control while attempting the rundown.
3. Not forcing the runner back by charging the runner.
4. Hitting the runner with the ball when throwing.

Teaching tips and strategy

1. Proper positioning, backing up, charging the runner and throwing accurately must be emphasized.
2. To eliminate the chance of a throwing error, fielders should attempt to tag the runner in two or less throws. The fielder who is to make the tag should

move toward the runner and call for the ball when within tagging range.

3. Fielders should force the runner to retreat toward the base previously passed and make the tag on the runner's back.
4. Fielders participating in a rundown should position themselves slightly to the side of the base path to allow a throwing lane.
5. Before throwing the ball, fielders should force the runner to commit to a particular direction.
6. Care must be taken to prevent other runners from advancing. When attempting a rundown on a player off of first base, a runner on third should not be allowed to score. The second baseman charges the runner near first and either tags or tosses the ball to the first baseman for the putout. The tag is made and the fielder immediately checks the runner or throws to home plate for the tag. If the runner on third is quick and has a good lead off the base, the best option may be to prevent both runners from advancing rather than trying for an out. In this case the second baseman forces the runner back to first while watching the other runner on third.

Drills

Rundown. A runner is stationed halfway between first and second base. Basemen are positioned on each bag. The b. all starts at first base and is thrown to second. Players will attempt a rundown. This drill also may be practiced between second and third, and third and home. Outfielders and pitchers not acting as fielders in the rundown may serve as trapped runners.

Fielding the bunt

Infielders must be able to anticipate bunting situations, and have a plan of action for fielding the ball or covering a base without hesitation.

Performance description

1. Anticipating the bunt, the first and third basemen charge toward the batter as the ball is pitched. As the ball reaches the plate, assume a ready position.

3. The ball is quickly scooped up, or barehanded, and a sidearm throw is made.

4. Second baseman and shortstop cover appropriate bases for putout attempts.

Common errors

1. Confusion in determining which player should field the bunt.

2. Failure to properly field a spinning ball.

3. Hesitating too long before deciding where to make the play.

Teaching tips and strategy

1. With the first and third basemen charging in, the second baseman covers first base and the shortstop covers second base. The left fielder may then cover third base for any play at that bag.

2. Know the bunting ability and speed of opponents and learn to anticipate bunting situations.

3. The fielder of the bunt should throw to the appropriate base, rather than throwing to the fielder who is moving to cover the base.

4. Attempts should be made to put out the lead

runner. If a lead runner putout is doubtful, the fielder should play for the sure out.

Drills

Bunt coverage. First and third basemen assume close-in positions. When the ball is pitched, a batter attempts to hit a bunt either down the first baseline, the third baseline or in front of the plate. Each batter attempts five bunts. On each bunt the fielders practice charging the ball or assuming their base covering positions. Baserunners may be added to this drill to simulate game situations.

Cutoff

Generally, players need much practice and experience to effectively decide whether or not a cutoff should be made. The purpose of the cutoff is to intercept and redirect a throw to put out a baserunner at a base other than the throw's original designation. Frequently, a player will cut off a throw to a base when it appears the throw will be unsuccessful in putting out a runner. By cutting off the ball, the fielder may prevent another runner from advancing, or may trap the advancing runner off base.

Performance description

1. A designated infielder calls for all cutoffs on throws from outfielders.

2. The cutoff player assumes a position approximately 20-25 feet in front of the intended target.

3. The cutoff player judges the possible success of the throw. If unsuccessful, the fielder intervenes and redirects the ball for another possibility.

Common errors

1. Cutting off a throw which could have resulted in a putout.
2. Failure to designate an infielder to call for cutoffs.

Teaching tips and strategy

I. Cutoffs on throws from right field to home are usually taken by the first baseman or pitcher. The player not executing the cutoff backs up home plate. Throws from left field to home are cut off by the pitcher or shortstop. The catcher, having a good view of the situation calls for the cutoff and redirection.

A catcher's throw to second base on stealing attempts may be cut off by the pitcher, second baseman, or shortstop when a runner is on third base. A good cutoff player throws immediately back to the catcher. Consequently, the runner at third may be trapped off the base for a putout, or the runner may be forced back to the base.

Drill

Cutoff. Defensive players take their respective positions in the field. The coach sets the situation by placing the runners on bases. As the batter hits a pitched ball, runners try to advance on base hits to the outfield. The catcher calls the plays: "Cut first," "cut second," or "cut third." "Cut" directs the cutoff player to catch the ball, and "first," "second," or "third" suggests the new direction for the throw. If a call is not made, the throw comes home uninterrupted.

Improving infield skills

The following complex drills offer new applications for

practicing strategic concepts and techniques previously introduced.

Drills

Wide throws to first. The coach or thrower takes a position two-thirds of the way to the shortstop position. Throws are alternated to the right and to the left of first base, forcing the baseman to stretch to make the catch.

Covering your bag. A ground ball is fungo hit to each infielder. The fielder throws the ball to first. The first baseman throws to the catcher. The catcher then throws to the base for which the infielder is responsible. The shortstop will cover second base upon return from the catcher. The ball is then thrown around the horn to the catcher. The process is repeated for each infielder.

Force play. The coach dictates a situation and the infielders take appropriate positions: normal, shallow, or deep. One runner is placed on first base. Additional runners are lined up outside the foul line at first base. The coach hits a ball to a fielder. The fielder executes a force play at second. Runners may be placed on first and second; or first, second, and third to increase the difficulty of the drill.

Stationary ball. Infielders are placed as indicated in the following diagram. Several softballs are placed six feet apart and ten feet in front of the infielder. The coach calls three numbers corresponding to positions in the infield. Example: The coach calls five, four, and three. The first number is the position of the player, and the second and third numbers indicate where the ball should be thrown. In this situation, the third baseman picks up one ball and throws to the second baseman who is covering second base. The second baseman then throws to the first baseman for a double play.

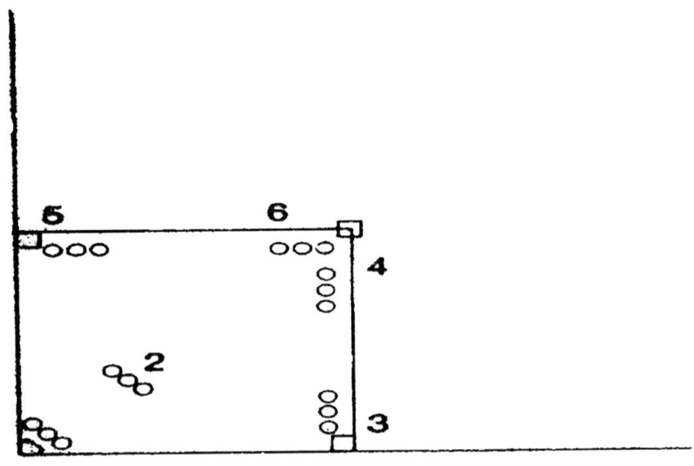

Fig. 2: Stationary ball

Multiple-ball box drill. The formation is basically the same as the one-ball box drill except the batter hits to a different fielder. The batter closest to third hits grounders to the fielder in shallow left field. The batter on the first base side of home plate hits grounders to the second baseman. The batter nearest first base hits to the fielder in shallow right field. The batter hits the second bail as the fielder throws the first ball to the catcher. The batter also place-hits the grounders to allow the fielder practice in lateral coverage.

The loop. Infielders line up at the third base coach's box. Fielders are positioned at first, second, and home. Several balls are placed on the ground two feet from the pitcher's plate on the third base side. An infielder takes a position at third base. The batter fungo hits a ground ball to the third baseman. The player fields the ball, throws to first base, runs to the mound, picks up the placed ball and throws to second. After the throw, the player runs the shortstop position, fields a looping fly ball (which has been hit or thrown by the coach), and throws it to the catcher.

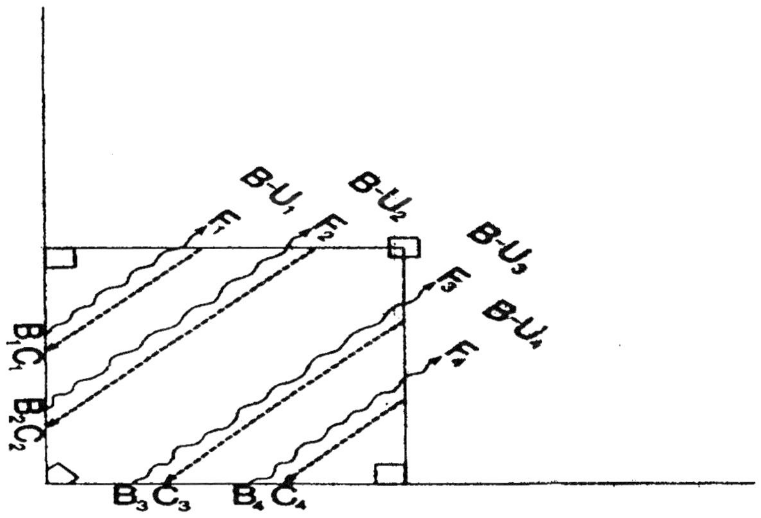

Fig. 3: Multiple-ball box drill

Continuous fielding. The batter fungo hits consecutive balls to the third baseman. Immediately following the throw to home another ball is hit to the fielder. The player continues to field the bail and throw to home until four fielding or throwing errors, or 20 successful plays have been made. Continue the drill with each position. Players should not try to pick up mishandled balls.

Suicide. The infielder assumes a normal fielding position. The batter hits I5 grounders in a row or as many as it takes for the fielder to make five consecutive plays without an error. Each play consists of a clean pick up and accurate throw to a designate base.

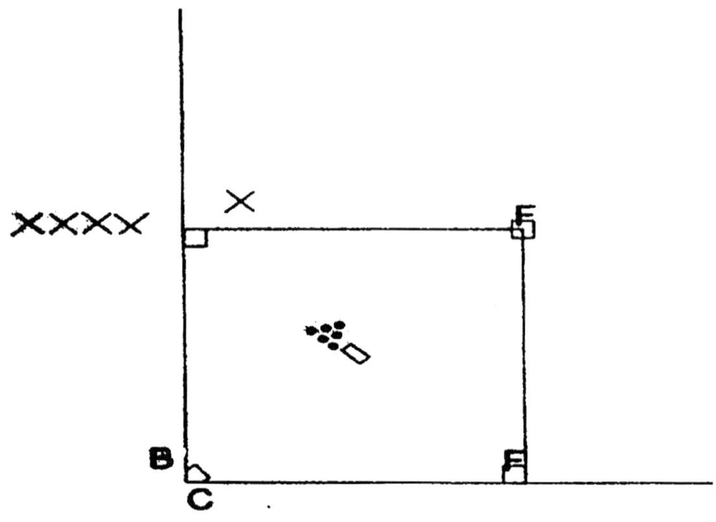

Fig. 4: The loop

Triple. The coach assigns players to infield positio with remaining players lining up as baserunne behind home plate. When the ball is hit, the runn sprints to first, rounds second, and runs to third. . the runner is running, the coach hits two balls in rap succession to the same infielder. The hits are timed the second hit is executed when the first throw is ma to first base, the third hit is made when the seco throw is made to second. As the runner rounds t bases, the first throw goes to first, the second thr goes to second, and the third throw goes to third ba The perfect play is an out at each base.

Running fungo. Players with their gloves on a stationed at second and third base. Other players, a with gloves on, line up at home. The first player runs at full speed to first base. As the runner rounds the base going to second, the coach hits a grounder between first and second. The runner fields the ball, throws to second and continues around second toward third. A second ball is hit between second and third. The runner fields the ball and throws it to third. The runner assumes the third baseman's position. The third baseman rotates to second base and the second baseman rotates to the end of the baserunner's line.

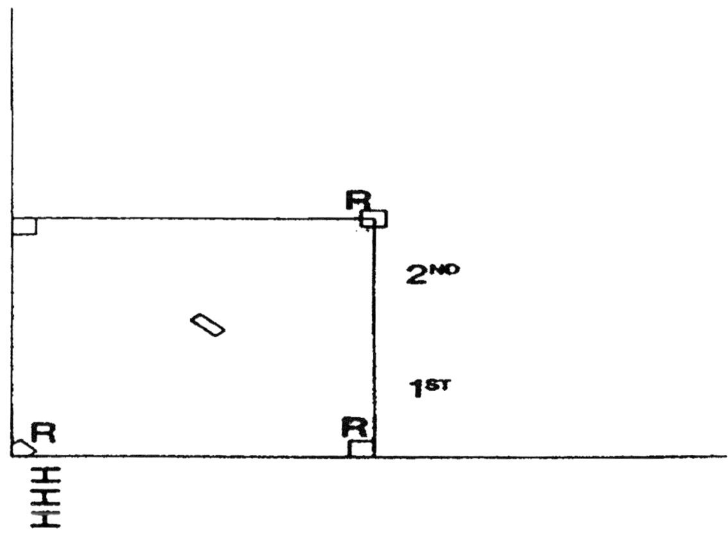

Fig. 5: Charge

Charge. Runners are placed at home, first base, and second base, with remaining runners lined up behind home facing first base. Fielders assume the first baseman and second baseman positions. Infielders line up one behind the other on first base side of home plate facing third base. When the coach calls "go," the first infielder on the first base line races for third.

When the infielder is midway between home and third, the runner on second breaks for third. Once at third base, the infielder turns to face the catcher who throws the ball to third. As the catch is made at third, the runner at first breaks for second base. The fielder makes the tag at third, throws to second, then runs across the diamond toward first base. The fielder at second makes the tag and holds the ball. As the infielder passes the pitcher's plate, the runner at home runs for first base. The coach hits a grounder just inside the first baseline. The infielder moving toward first base fields the ball, throws to first base for the out and goes to the end of the baserunners' line. Baserunners from second go to the end of the infielders' line. Upon completion of the play the runners at first and second remain on their base. A new runner takes a position at home.

Double triangle. The double triangle drill has four phases of infield practice. Batter, catcher, and infielders assume the described positions.

Phase 1. All infielders except the pitcher assume their respective positions. A batter and catcher assume positions, behind the baseline, halfway between home and first base. Another batter and catcher assume a comparable position on the third base line between home and third. The batter on the first base line fungo hits grounders to the shortstop who throws to first base. The ball is then returned to the appropriate catcher. The batter on the third base line fungo hits a ground ball to the second baseman who throws to the third baseman. The ball is then returned to the appropriate catcher.

Phase 2. The batter on the third base line hits a slow

grounder to the first baseman who fields the ball and throws to the shortstop covering second. The shortstop then returns the ball to the appropriate catcher. The batter on the first base line hits a slow grounder to the third baseman who fields the ball and then throws to the second baseman covering first base. The ball is then returned to the appropriate catcher.

Phase 3. The batter on the first base side hits to the shortstop who tosses the ball to the second baseman covering the bag. The second baseman returns the ball to the catcher. The batter on the third base line hits to the first baseman who throws to the third baseman on the base. The third baseman returns the ball to the catcher.

Phase 4. The batter on the first base line hits a grounder to the third baseman who throws to first. The first baseman returns the ball to catcher. The batter on the third base fine hits a ground ball to the second baseman who tosses the ball to the shortstop covering second. The shortstop returns the ball to catcher.

Outfield

Outfielders must be conditioned to execute correctly previously taught outfield skills, including positioning for the catch, backing up infielders, throwing to a relay player, and fielding deep hits. Instinctively, players should back up adjacent outfielders and charge forward on balls hit to infielders in front of them. Frequently they must serve as relay players to assist other fielders. Cooperation must exist between adjacent outfielders and between infielders and outfielders to prevent collisions and mishandling of the ball in overlap areas. In addition to judging the velocity and direction of a batted ball, outfielders must know their own speed and capabilities in determining whether a shoestring catch, or allowing the ball to bounce before the catch is more appropriate. Misjudging hardhit balls can result in an error which allows the runner more bases than deserved.

Performance description

1. When not involved in catching or backing up, move into a position for a possible relay on deep hits.
2. If it appears the baserunner will not advance beyond the base approached, and a play cannot be made on the runner, immediately bring the ball to throwing position and run toward the base to which the runner is advancing.
3. Throw the ball low to the base ahead of a runner when a tag is to be attempted. If it appears that the baserunner will advance beyond the base approached, throw to the next base closest to home.

Common esrrors

1. Not calling for balls hit between fielders or not heeding an adjacent fielder's call.
2. Throwing "behind the baserunner."
3. Failure to use good judgment regarding the choice between throwing the ball or running it into the infield.

Teaching tips and strategy

1. Appropriate signals should be taught to all fielders to eliminate confusion on balls hit between them.

Drills

Shoestring catches. Outfielders line up in center field. The coach and catcher stand on the left field foul line. On signal, the fielder runs directly toward the coach. The coach throws a low, sinking line drive directly at the fielder. The fielder catches, blocks, or traps the ball and throws it to the catcher.

Charge, scoop, throw. Outfielders line up in single file at one outfield position or take their respective positions in the outfield. The ball is batted to the fielder from the pitcher's plate. Charging the ball at top speed, the outfielder assumes a position in line with the target to which the ball is to be thrown. The ball is caught and an overhand throw is made without losing the forward momentum. Baserunners may be used to make the drill more realistic.

Tag-up throw. Runners line up in the third base coaching box. One runner takes a position at third base. Fielders assume normal positions. A coach fungo hits a fly into short left field. The fielder makes the catch and throws the ball home in an attempt to put out the runner who advances on the catch. This procedure is continued for all fielders.

Non-stop. Batter hits 20 consecutive balls to the outfielder. The player fields the ball and throws in the following pattern: first ball is thrown home; second ball is thrown to third; third ball is thrown to second; and fourth ball is thrown to first. Basemen return all balls to catcher. Each hit is made simultaneously with the throw from the previous catch. A prompter may be used to remind the fielder where to throw the ball. The catcher counts the hits and keeps the batter supplied with balls.

All the way. Outfielders line up in foul territory perpendicular to the third base line 15 yards past the base. The first fielder runs into left field as the ban is hit into mid-left field. The fielder catches the ball and throws to home and continues to run toward center field. The second hit is to left-center field. The fielder makes the catch, throws to home, and continues to run toward center field. The third hit is to right-center field. The fielder makes the catch, throws home and continues running. The fourth hit is to right field. The fielder makes the catch and throws home. The fielder then runs out-of-bounds at the right field line and waits there until the other fielders complete the drill. When all fielders are at the right field line, the procedure is reversed to move toward the left field line.

Six-man slam. This drill involves hitting, fielding, and throwing. Fielders are stationed in left, center, and right field. A cutoff player is stationed approximately midway between the fielders and the batter. A catcher is stationed beside the batter and directs the cutoff player to a proper position as the batter hits to left field. The batter then fungo hits the next ban to center field and so on. Players rotate one position after each batter has hit balls to every fielder twice.

Batting

Bunting

In fast-pitch softball, having players who can bunt the ball gives a team a vital offensive weapon. A bunt is a surprise tactic frequently used when infielders are playing deep in their positions. More often bunting is employed to draw the first baseman and third baseman in, close to the plate, when a runner is on base, usually first. With the baserunner advancing on the pitch, the fielder has insufficient time to make a successful play on the runner and must throw to first base for the putout * Moreover, with the first and third basemen and pitcher charging in, confusion in fielding the bunt, or covering the bases, may result in a defensive error. Thus, the properly executed sacrifice bunt safely places a baserunner in scoring position. Likewise, the squeeze bunt, which requires a highly competent batter, may be used to advance a fast runner from third to home. The deceptive fake bunt is most appropriately employed when a runner is stealing third base. This manuever draws the third baseman in and away from the base and may distract the catcher, thus delaying, the quick throw to the bag. A slap hit may be used to pull the defense in close to assist a baserunner in stealing or to allow the batter to hit the ball just over the charging infielder's head.

Performance description

1. Grip bat firmly with the bottom hand,
2. Support bat loosely with the top hand sliding to a position midway up the bat. Place the thumb on top, with the fingers supporting under, and parallel to, the bat (away from the hitting surface).
3. As the ball is released, pivot, with feet slightly apart, to face the pitcher.
4. Square the shoulders and position the bat parallel, or at a slight angle, to the ground.
5. Angle bat with top hand on contact to direct the ball to the right, left, or center.
6. "Give" with the arms and bat while contacting the ball in front of the plate.

7. To execute a drag bunt, assume a normal batting stance, without stride, and tap the ball down the appropriate baseline. Right-handed batters should direct the ball down the third base line, and left-handed batters should place it down the first base line.
8. To execute a slap hit, during the wind-up assume a bunting position, then quickly assume a normal batting position. Bring the bat back quickly and swing at the ball.
9. To fake bunt, assume a bunting position deep in the batter's box, but do not contact the ball.

Common errors

1. Placing the top hand's fingers around the bat, vulnerable to the oncoming ball.
2. Failure to "give with the ball" on contact.
3. Popping the ball up in the air due to failure to contact the ball squarely with the bat.
4. Failure to disguise the bunt prior to release of the pitch.
5. On a sacrifice or squeeze bunt, failure to contact the ball.

Teaching tips and strategy

1. Low pitches are easiest to bunt.
2. To promote "giving" upon contact, players should "catch the ball with the bat."
3. Players should practice directing the ball down opposite foul lines.
4. Generally, bunters should go with the pitch. Inside

pitches should be bunted toward first base and outside pitches toward third.

5. A fake hit may be followed with a slap hit. Once infielders are drawn in, a slap hit will direct the ball just over their heads. The slap hit is made with a short, quick backswing.
6. To advance a runner to second, a bunt is hit in the direction of the fielder who would have the most difficult throw to second.
7. The sacrifice bunt should be used when there are no outs, the game is close or runners are on first, first and second, or second base.

Drills

Bunting drill. Four players participate in this drill: a pitcher, two fielders, and a batter. One fielder is positioned on the first base line and the other fielder on the third base line. The batter bunts eight or ten pitched balls, after which players rotate one position clockwise.

Reaction bunting. At close range a pitcher throws overhand to a batter, who attempts to bunt the ball in designated directions. Ten attempts are allowed each batter.

Squeeze bunt drill. Infielders assume a "close in" position with a runner on third base. A pitched ball is bunted to the ground and the runner attempts to advance. If the ball is popped up the runner returns to third. Pitcher, catcher, first and third basemen all move to play the bunted ball. The direction of the bunt will be varied in successive attempts.

Place hitting

Once the basic batting technique is mastered a batter must strive to place hit the ball into open areas of the field, down the foul fines, or between fielders. By adjusting the point of contact, the stance, or the follow-through, the batter may be able to direct the ball toward less skilled players, or hit behind a runner to permit further advancement.

Performance description

1. From normal batting position, move the forward foot to an open or closed stance.
2. Hit to the opposite field by closing the stance, swinging "late," and letting the follow-through angle the bat toward the desired field.
3. To pull a ball, open the stance, contact the ball in front of the body, break the wrists sharply, and forcefully follow through.
4. To hit the ball straight away, or to center field, assume a normal stance and make contact with the ball when it is even with the forward hip.
5. For hitting a greater distance, use along grip, swing forcefully and follow through slightly upward.

Common errors

1. Failure to consider location of the pitch in determining the place hitting direction.
2. Improper execution in "hitting behind" a runner to the opposite field.
3. Attempting to hit a long ball instead of place-hitting safely.

4. Stepping across the plate or out of the batter's box before making contact.

Teaching tips and strategy

1. "Choking up" on fast balls permits a quicker, more controlled swing.
2. Right-handed batters should pull inside pitches to left field and hit outside pitches to right field
3. Hitting behind the runner" places the ball away from the direction of the advancing runner.

Drills

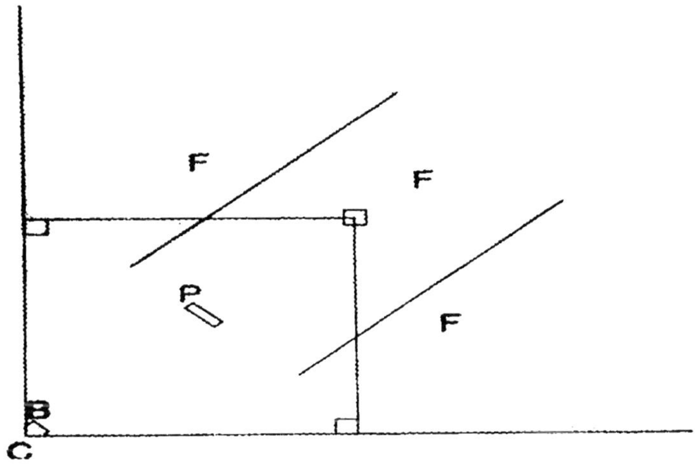

Fig. 6: Place hitting

Place hitting. Mark off a zone of 15 feet on each side of second base. Six players (three fielders, one pitcher, one catcher, and one batter) are involved in the drill. Each batter has six swings. The object is to score the most points. One point is scored for each hit into the target zone. The players should rotate after the batter completes six swings. Zones may be established in any field.

Fungo hitting

One technique that utilizes the fundamentals of place hitting is fungo hitting. Fungo hitting may develop batting strength and improve eye-hand coordination. Although not used in actual play, the skill is appropriate for hitting balls to infielders or outfielders in practice or warm-up situations.

Performance description

1. Hold the ball in the non-dominant hand, waist high, in front of the body.
2. With the dominant hand, grasp the bat approximately six to ten inches up the grip and hold the bat back and away from the shoulder.
3. Toss the ball upward and approximately four feet from the body.
4. Immediately place the non-dominant hand below the other hand on the grip.
5. Keep the eye on the ball, and time the full swing tc meet the ball as it drops.
6. Follow through.

Common errors

1. Not placing the nondominant hand on the bat.
2. Not tossing the ball far enough away from the bod) or at a sufficient height to allow for a full swing,

Drills

1. Practice hitting balls to designated infielders o: outfielders.
2. Using the fungo technique, apply the place hittin; drill.

Improving batting skills

The following drills add game-like elements to practicing batting skills.

Drills

Rotational batting. Three teams of five players each are formed. Team A is at bat. Team B positions a battery, first baseman, second baseman, and right fielder to the right side of the field. Team C positions the third baseman, shortstop, left fielder, center fielder, and short fielder to the left side of the field. Team A attempts to score against teams B and C. Team A bats until three outs are made. Team B then bats as Team A rotates to the left side of the field, and Team C rotates to the right side of the field and furnishes the battery. Play continues until each team has had a turn at bat.

Four-player team. An offensive team consisting of four players attempts to score against a full defensive team. Players continue their turn at bat until three outs are made.

Baserunning

A thorough knowledge of running bases will undoubtedly earn extra runs for a team. Batters and baserunners should be aware of each situation and follow appropriate baserunning patterns. Advanced instruction should include the proper use of the leadoff, hit and run, steal and slide.

Leadoff

In fast pitch softball, the baserunner should lead off the base as soon as the ball leaves the pitcher's hand. The leadoff should be the greatest distance that allows the baserunner to return to the base safely in case of a pickoff attempt. Slow pitch rules do not allow th player to leave the base until the ball crosses home plate or is hit.

Performance description

I. Assume a takeoff position facing the next base with body low and weight forward.

2. Place the left foot in a push-off position on the inside corner of the base.

3. Without hesitation, take several steps off the base at the moment permitted by the rules.

4. As the lead-off is taken, focus the eyes on home plate to determine if the ball is hit or misplayed by the catcher.

5. If the ball is thrown back to the pitcher and no opportunity for stealing is present, quickly return to the base and repeat the process on the next pitch.

6. Alternate method:

    a. Place the left foot on the base with the right foot behind the base.

    b. Step forward with the rear foot prior to the pitcher's release (fast pitch).

Common errors

1. Leading off the base too soon.

2. Failure to return to the base quickly when a steal is not attempted, resulting in being trapped between bases.

3. Underestimating or overestimating personal capabilities and speed in taking a leadoff.

Teaching tips and strategy

1. After leading off, advance without hesitation when a ground ball is Wt.
2. On a line drive, the runner should delay the advance to see if the ball is caught. If the ball is not caught, the runner should proceed rapidly. If caught, a quick return to the base must be made. Players must be alert to opportunities to tag up and run.
3. Runners must know the greatest distance a leadoff may be taken safely. Due to the throwing distance from home to second base, a longer leadoff may be taken from second than from other bases.
4. If a long fly ball is hit, the runner should take a lengthy leadoff and observe if the ball is caught or in play; then advance or return to the base. If the runner is on second or third bases, a coach may assist by signalling to return or advance,
5. With less than two outs, on a shallow-hit ball to a fielder with a strong throwing arm, faking a sprint home can draw the throw.
6. Lead-offs from third base should be taken in foul territory to avoid the runner being struck by a fair ball.

Drills

Leadoff. Players assume fielding positions. Runner on first base practices leading off when the ball is pitched. If the ball is a base hit, the runner quickly reacts by running to the next base. If the ball is caught, the runner returns to the base.

Hit-and-Run

The hit-and-run is a predetermined play in which the baserunner advances with the expectation that the batter will hit the ball. The batter's intent is to hit the ball into an area vacated by a fielder moving to cover the base to which the baserunner is advancing. Frequently, the play is used with a runner on first to advance the runner of two bases. The fast takeoff gives the runner an advantage in reaching the bases safely and limits the double play possibility. The hit-and-run is effective in scoring a runner from third when the fielders are moving in anticipation of a squeeze bunt. A prerequisite for the hit-and-run is a fast runner and a dependable batter who can hit hard ground balls.

Performance description

1. The hit-and-run signal is given by the third-base coach.
2. On the pitch, the baserunner charges to the next base.
3. As the baseman moves to cover the base of the advancing runner, the batter hits to the baseman's original position.

Common errors

1. Batter does not attempt to hit the pitch.
2. Batter hits a sharp line drive which is caught by a fielder who then puts out the baserunner for a double play.
3. Ball is popped up on an infield fly.
4. Baserunner hesitates after leaving the base.

Teaching tips

1. Preferably the batter should hit a ground ball,

Drill

Baserunner's suicide. The entire team lines up single file at home plate. Using a staggered start, all players sprint to first base as if a single had been hit. After all players reach first base, players individually assume a baserunner's position, Players then advance on the coach's command and stop on third base. As baserunners on third, players sprint home. From the home plate position, runners advance to second base as if a, double were hit, then sprint directly home. The drill continues as runners go for a triple, and finally for a home run. It is important that all baserunners maintain a staggered start throughout the drill. Using runners only on first or third, this drill may be used to practice the hit-and-run.

Stealing

Base stealing is a technique which advances runners into better scoring positions through speed, alertness, and cunning. Instruction in the appropriate opportunities and techniques of stealing will enhance success. A baserunner who is a stealing threat is often distracting to a pitcher and catcher and may cause a loss of concentration on the pitch. Consequently, the threat alone can force errors by the defensive team. Good baserunners analyze the pitcher, catcher, and infielders for weaknesses in protecting against the steal, and take advantage of any vulnerabilities.

Performance description

1. From a leadoff position on base, sprint toward the next base without hesitation as the ball is pitched.

2. If the play is made to the base approached, slide.

Common errors

1. Not breaking quickly from the base.
2. Watching the ball instead of focusing the eyes ahead.
3. Hesitating after initially leaving the base.

Teaching tips and strategy

1. A delayed steal may be attempted by swift runners:
   a. After the leadoff on a pitch, if the catcher does not force the runner back to the base, the runner should advance as the ball is thrown back to the pitcher.
   b. With runners on first and third bases, and less than two outs, the runner on first base takes a long leadoff to draw a throw. The runner advances if the throw is made to first or no throw is attempted. If the throw is made to second, the runner retreats to first, or stops momentarily attempting to draw the fielder's attention and allowing the runner on third to score.
2. Double stealing may be effective and distracting to the opponents. With runners on first and third and less than two outs, both runners break and advance simultaneously.
3. Good strategy includes stealing if the catcher has a weak throwing arm or a slow delivery, and if infielders do not cover their bases properly.
4. Avoid overrunning other baserunners.

Drills

Double-steal drill. Runners are positioned on first and third bases. As the pitcher delivers to the catcher, the runners attempt to advance. The catcher then makes a play on either runner.

Continuous stealing. With players in the field, a runner is placed on first base. As the pitcher releases the ball to a batter, the runner is instructed to steal on a particular pitch or allowed to make an individual decision. Whether safe or out, the runner assumes a position on second and attempts to steal third. Once at third, the runner attempts to steal home. The batter does not attempt to hit any pitches.

Sliding

An advanced player should slide on close plays at any base except when advancing to first. The slide reduces the target for a fielder's tag, and prevents the baserunner from overrunning second or third base without losing speed in the approach. Three commonly used slides will be described. The straight-leg slide has the basic low, straight in approach to the bag. If in doubt about the closeness of the play; the bent-leg slide is recommended. Upon completion of this slide, the runner is standing and ready to advance to the next base. In order to avoid a tag, the hook slide is made to one side of the base,

Performance description

I. Straight-leg slide

   a. Initiate the slide approximately ten feet from the base.

   b. Lean back, and extend either leg forward and upward.

c. Bend the other leg at the knee under the extended leg.

d. Slide along the ground on the bottom leg and hip.

e. Keep the forward leg and arms off the ground,

2. Bent-leg slide

a. Initiate the slide about five feet from the base.

b. Check the backward fall.

c. Bend the nonsliding, forward leg at the knee,

d. Bend the sliding leg under the other leg.

e. As soon as the forward leg touches the bag, thrust the arms and body weight forward, and push the body upward with the sliding leg to a standing position.

3. Hook slide

a. Initiate the slide with either foot, as in the straight-leg slide.

b. Lean backward.

c. Turn the body to the side away from the tag.

d. Bend the knee of the leg nearest the base and hook the base with the toes.

Common errors

1. Catching the cleats in the ground while sliding.
2. Falling back on the hands, wrists and fingers resulting in possible injury.
3. Initiating the slide too early or late.

Teaching tips and strategy

1. For safety purposes, players should wear long pants or long socks when practicing or playing.
2. Know where to start the slide in relation to the bases.
3. Once the slide is started, continue until completion.
4. Flatten the body while going down to prevent sliding abrasions.
5. Watch the base and not the ball.
6. Keep hands closed on the slide.

Drills

Soft sliding. Using proper technique, players may practice sliding on a grassy area, in a sand pit, or on a tumbling mat.

Repeated slides. Players line up ten feet from a base. Individually, players take the appropriate number of steps and go into a sliding position. The distance and speed of the slide is gradually increased with each attempt.

6

CONDITIONING

Proper conditioning is a key element in preparing players to perform safely and efficiently. In addition, experienced teachers and coaches recognize the importance of warming up prior to a session of active drill participation. To aid in the physical development and bodily preparedness of a softball player, a conditioning program should stress the following components of fitness: strength, agility, flexibility, and endurance. The exercises presented in this chapter have been selected and organized according to these components. The simplicity and adaptability of the exercises make them suitable for a variety of programs and conditioning levels of the participants. Although an attempt has been made to designate suitability for class or competitive teams, certain exercises may be adaptable to both. Obviously, time will be a factor in determining the number of exercises to be included in each session. However, the instructor should attempt to encompass at least one exercise from each component group.

Exercises for class instruction

Strength

Pull-ups. Using an overhand grip, place both hands, shoulder width apart, on a horizontal bar. Raise the body until the chin is above the level of the bar. Lower the body to the starting position. Repeat three to five times.

Bent knee situps. Assume a bent knee position with hands placed on shoulders. Lower the body to the ground. Raise the body until the nose touches the knees. Do as many as possible in 60 seconds.

Modified push-ups. From a hands and knees position, bend the arms and lower trunk to touch the chin to the ground. Raise back up to starting position. Repeat 25 times. Regulation push-ups may be used by assuming a prone position with weight distributed on hands and feet.

Agility

Shuttle run. Repeat two or three runs to a designated line, 60 feet from the starting line, and back to the start. Option: From a fielding position use a side shuffle step to alternate touches between the two lines. Repeat 50 times.

Footwork. Stand with feet shoulder-width apart, knees bent and body weight distributed on the, balls of both feet. On the instructor's command move right, left, forward, or backward. Change direction as smoothly and quickly as possible.

Flexibility

Straddle sit stretches. Sitting with legs in straddle position, touch head to left knee and sustain the stretch for approximately five seconds. Repeat the process, touching head to right knee. Perform three times to each side. *Option:* Use hurdle-sitting position to perform stretches.

Stride standing. From a standing position, bend trunk to right, left, forward, and backward, holding each position for five seconds.

Windmill. Prom a stride-standing position, twist trunk to the left and touch right hand to left foot. Return to starting position and twist trunk to the right until left hand touches right foot. Repeat this action five times to each side.

Foot to hand. Lie on back with arms extended out to sides at shoulder height. Lift right foot and touchs to left hand. Keep shoulders and back flat on the ground. Return to starting position and touch left foot to right hand. Repeat five times to each side.

Endurance

Arm circles. With arms extended at sides and palms turned downward, rotate arms forward, making large circles 50 times. Turn palms upward and rotate extended arms backwards 50 times.

Bench step. Facing a bench 12-inches high, step up with right foot, left foot, then down with right foot and left foot respectively. Repeat for 60 seconds.

Exercise for competitive teams

Strength

Isometric rope pull. Tie the end of a five-foot rope to a stationary object at approximately waist height. Tie the other end of the rope to the throwing hand. Sustain a pull against the rope for six seconds from the following positions: in the overarm throw, back, release point, and follow through. Repeat two more times, allowing for rest between effort.

Isometric squeeze. Squeeze a tennis ball in each hand for

eight seconds using maximum effort. Repeat three times.

Isometric bat drill. Player assumes a batting stance. At backswing position, resistance is maintained on the bat in the opposite direction of the swing by a teammate. Both individuals maintain opposing pressure for eight seconds. Players rest for five seconds, and the bat is moved to the straight arm position and held at that spot for resistance. Proper wrist position must be maintained throughout the swing. This process is continued with the follow-through phase of the swing. Again, positions are held with resistance for eight seconds.

Isometric throw. Player assumes a bent elbow throwing position. Partner places left hand under elbow of player and right hand grasps player's wrist. Partner resists and the player holds a maximum contraction for ten seconds attempting to force hand forward and down.

Weight windup. Attach a string supporting a five-pound weight to the center of a broom handle. Using an overhand grip, rotate the handle to wind string around it until the weight is raised to the top. Repeat a minimum of three times.

Agility

Lateral jump. Balance a dowel rod between two upright concrete blocks, Jump back and forth across the rod as many times as possible in 30 seconds.

Flexibility

Prior to team participation, the athlete should, slowly and smoothly, perform static stretching exercises. In each of the exercises the student reaches the maximum stretch position and holds that position for a designated time not exceeding one minute. Through these flexibility exercises, chances of injury are decreased and the muscles are prepared for the stress which will follow. Jerking and bobbing motions should be eliminated from the movement.

Wall exercise. Assume a position with back to a wall. With thigh parallel to the floor, move down the wall as if sitting in a chair. Hold this position to stretch the quadriceps.

Gastronemics exercise. To stretch the gastronernics., assume a standing position facing a wall three feet away. Extend arms to wall to support body. With heels remaining flat on the floor and back straight, press body toward wall by bending the elbows. Hold at a 65-degree angle.

Shoulder stretching. Assume a standing position with feet shoulder-width apart. The arms are extended Straight in front of the body. With the fingers interlaced, raise the arms overhead while reversing the hand position. Force straight arms back as far as possible while the chin remains tucked. Hold this position, stretching the shoulders.

Endurance

Bleacher run. Taking one step at a time, players run up 15 rows of bleachers and back down. Repeat for 12 minutes.

Jump rope. Jump off both feet turning rope as rapidly as possible for 60 seconds.

Weight training

Weight training uses a series of progressive resistive exercises designed to develop strength and endurance. Exercises for the entire body, working through a full range of motion, should be included in a program. Both isotonic contraction (muscle fibers shorten) and eccentric contraction (muscle fibers lengthen) are involved in moving the weights. Isometric exercises (no shortening of muscle fibers) may be combined with a weight training program for rapid strength development. If isometrics are used, contractions should be held for eight seconds, with only one set per day recommended.

The duration of a weight training session should be 45 minutes to one hour in length. In setting up the program, each muscle group involved must be mechanically analyzed. Players should be pretested and tested periodically throughout the program to determine, their maximum effort. The program should be utilized three times weekly while in pre-season training and twice a week during the season. All sessions should be preceded by a general warm-up. Records should be kept for each individual to assure proper progression.

For strength development, an overload principle is applied so the muscle is working against resistance, greater than that to which it is accustomed. Weights should be heavy enough so that only four or five repetitions are possible. The last set for the workout should employ weights of maximum.

For muscular-endurance development, the weight load for the initial set of an exercise should be heavy enough to allow only ten to 12 repetitions, The first three repetitions must be done smoothly and slowly to warm the muscle groups adequately. The second set weight load should allow only eight or nine repetitions. The final set uses weights which make more than seven repetitions impossible. An adequate interval between sets should be established.

Beach press (arm endurance and strength). Lie flat on bench or floor. Grasp barbell at straight-arm, length above chest. Inhale deeply and lower barbell, with control, to chest. Do not pause when barbell reaches chest, but immediately exhale and raise barbell to original position. Keep feet flat on the floor and do not bridge back.

Calf raise (leg endurance and strength). Begin at standing position with barbell resting on back of shoulders. Rise on balls of feet and return to starting position. A block of wood under the balls of the feet increases the range of movement in the lower leg muscles.

Situps (abdominal endurance aid strength). Lie on an inclined plane with head at lower end, knees bent, and feet secured in place. Hold dumbbells on each shoulder throughout the exercise.

Barbell rowing (shoulder and arm endurance and strength). From a standing position, bend upper body forward until back is parallel to the floor. Flex knees slightly for comfort and balance. Grip barbell using an overhand grip, arms shoulder width apart. Lift barbell from floor and raise to chest, elbows close to body. Inhale when raising barbell from the floor and exhale when lowering it.

Leg bicep curls (leg endurance and strength). Lie face

down on an inclined plan with head at tipper end and weights on ankles. Inhale and flex legs until feet are close to hips. Exhale and slowly lower legs to starting position.

Dumbbell lateral raise (arm and chest endurance and strength). Start in bench press position, dumbbell in each hand facing one another. From this straight-arm position slowly lower dumbbells out to a position slightly below level of body. Inhale when lowering dumbbells and exhale when returning to starting position.

Behind the neck press (shoulder and arm endurance and strength). Grip barbell with wider grip than usual. Lift barbell from floor to resting position on shoulders. Inhale and press barbell until arms are extended overhead, Exhale and slowly lower barbell to position on shoulders. Do each repetition without resting.

Back extension (back and shoulder endurance and strength). Perform on high table or exercise bench. Lie on stomach with legs on bench and upper body over end of bench, hips forward. Partner holds legs. Grasp hands behind neck. Exhale and lower the upper body toward floor until body is in pike position. Inhale and raise tipper body to position level with legs.

7

CLASS ORGANISATION

The goal of class organization is to structure the learning experiences so as to be meaningful to the students. Effective teachers and coaches realize the importance of good organization as it relates to safety, instruction, grouping, use of student leaders, and skill development. Factors which influence the organization of a class include the philosophy of the teacher, the objectives of the program, the number of leaders, the number of players, the size of the facilities, the availability of equipment, and the skill and interest level of the players.

Safety

When assuming liability for the welfare of students, the softball teacher must exercise forethought, good judgment, and adhere to sound safety practices. Good class organization helps to insure the safety of the players. Safety must be stressed in conditioning, warm-up activities, offensive and defensive techniques, and actual play. Policies should be made and strictly observed. The following are examples of safety procedures which might be employed:

1. In throwing and catching warm-up drills involving parallel lines:

a. Adjacent players should be a safe distance from each other and equidistant from their partners.

b. If the ball is missed, the player should retrieve the ball and return to the line before throwing it to the partner. This practice eliminates the hazards of making long inaccurate throws which might endanger unsuspecting players that are engaged in the drill.

c. The first pair in the formation should take a position furthest from the equipment basket or instructional area, allowing subsequent partners to line up without walking behind or in front of those throwing.

2. Players should never throw the ball unless a target is made by the receiver.
3. Players should swing bats only when involved in a drill, or in areas designated by the leader. The designated swinging and batting areas are off-limits to all other players.
4. Specific areas should be assigned for teams and players waiting their turn at bat.
5. Injuries must be promptly reported to the instructor.
6. All equipment in need of repair must be reported to the instructor.
7. Players must be required to wear proper safety equipment,
8. After hitting the ball, the bat should be dropped never slung or thrown

9. When instruction is being given, players should hold the ball or put it on the ground.
10. Facilities should be properly maintained and be free from hazards that may cause injury.
11. Players should not be required to play when weather conditions are dangerous.

Instructional techniques

Poorly organized classes result in player apathy, which is frequently exemplified by a lack of motivation, "hustle," and attendance. The astute leader will give thoughtful attention to effective Instructional techniques.

With respect to timing anti sequence, there are several considerations to keep in mind. Verbal instruction should be succinct. Usually players are eager to participate and become restless when kept inactive for long periods of time. The presentation of information should be organized in a logical, progressive sequence. During each session, time should be allotted for instruction, drills, practice and play, if appropriate. Each session should focus on key points to be learned with time provided for players to learn a new skill or improve existing skills. New material should be presented early in the session while players are attentive. If suitable, the session should end with an enjoyable game in which the skills that have been learned are applied. The game may be a contest, a lead-up game, or a modified game.

Audio-visual aids

Video tape or films allow students to see themselves in action. In addition to being an enjoyable activity, these viewings can also be valuable in pointing out the players' strengths and weaknesses. Other visual aids such as movies, loop films, and charts depicting skills or rules are useful in stimulating interest.

Use of student leaders

Student leaders can assist the teacher or coach in several ways. They can serve as peer teachers, role models for other students, or as officials, coaches, and statisticians. Additionally, they may monitor activities by directing drills, conducting warm-ups, and acting as station leaders in circuit training. Administratively, student leaders may assist it: roll check, equipment accountability and facility inspection. Care must be taken to avoid exploitation of these valuable assistants. At no time should they be held responsible for conducting the class or practice, or assume a substitute teaching role. A leadership training program may be instituted to train students for these positions and develop their leadership skills.

Coping with the environment

Conditions in the environment often influence the effectiveness of instruction. Factors such as other activities on the field, noise, temperature, wind, field condition, and position of the sun require special attention when instructing the group.

As a general rule the players should not look into the sun while receiving instruction. Sometimes, however, the sun may be less distracting to the players than facing activities which compete for their attention. Good voice projection is vital to being heard and to keeping the group's attention.

During instruction, players should be infront of and facing the leader. When possible, the instructor should enhance voice projection by not talking in to the wind. A whistle may be used to signal a change of activities or to call the group together for instruction. When the whistle is blown, players should stop aft activity and listen for diretions. Indiscriminate or, too frequent use of the whistle reduces the signal's effectiveness.

Throughout Instruction, especially with the beginning groups, the leader should be mindful of left-handed players. It is often helpful to these players if the teacher, or a skilled left-handed student, is capable of demonstrating movement or the entire skill with the left hand. However, if the leader is right-handed', this may be difficullt, Wfin, possible, instructions should exclude the words "right" and "left'. Instead, use descriptive terms such as "front foot," "back foot." When using lineformation for practicing such as swinging a bat, the left-handed players should be placed to the far right as the instructor views the line.

Dividing the group into squads in commonly used technique for organizing players into manageable units for instruction. Another approach, squad formaltion expedites and facilities roll call, instruction, and drill practice. Generally, six players are assigned to a group for instruction and drills. Larger squads usually result in players having fewer opportunities for practice. For learns or drills requiring more players, squads may combined. Several methods for cassifying students into squads include: skill or motor tests, age or experience, physical fitness level, student choice, Players may be homogeneously or heterogeneously grouped.

By grouping hornogeneously, instruction can be directed to every player in that group since their abilities and their progression are basically the same. In addition, feelings of inadequacy within the groups are minimized as players are participating with those of similar ability. However, homogeneous grouping has some disadvantages. If groups are forced to compete against each other, the lower skilled groups may become discouraged. Also the leader-ship within a particular group may be lacking.

Heterogeneous grouping also has advantages and disadvantages. One advantage is that the groups are approximately equal in ability, which facilitates game play. Heterogeneous grouping provides opportunities for the highly skilled to assist to their less adept teammates. Social development is enhanced as students relate to others with different abilites. A disadvantage of heterogeneous grouping is that some students may be intimidated, as the result of being placed in groups where other students are of superior ability. In addition it is often difficult for the instructor to plan drills and practice sessions challenging to all players in hetrogeneous group.

One approach for consideration is to homogeneously group the class for skill development and heterogeneously group the class for garne play. This allows the instructor to capitalize on the strengths of each method of grouping.

At times the leader may feel the purpose of the activity are best served by allowing the students to choose their own teams. When this is done, it is best for captains to meet with the teacher and select the groups in private. The players should not the order in which they were chosen. Leaders may determine that a less structured approach is appropriate, and instruct the students to count-off to form the groups. In this procedure, students line tip arid count-off in pairs or groups of threes, fours, fives, etc. If the leader is seeking heterogeneous grouping through this approach, care should be taken to see that students do not arrange themselves in line in order to get in the squad they desire.

8

MODIFIED SOFTBALL GAMES

When introducing basic skills to young players, the use of lead-up games combines skill practice with the enjoyment of game play. By emphasizing correct form in executing the particular skills required for each game, the instructor is afforded a motivational supplement to drill practice. During the early skill developmental stages, repeated skill applications provide the necessary foundation for later regulation game play.

Twenty one. (Develops throwing, baserunning, and fielding skills) With all fielders in regular fielding positions, the batter throws the ball overhand into fair territory. Following the throw, the batter runs and touches as many bases as possible before a fielder makes a tag with the ball or touches the base to which the runner is advancing. The runner must continue running until being put out or reaching home base. A point is scored for each base the runner successfully passes. With each new batter, the fielders rotate one position. After every member of' the team bats, the teams change places. The first team to attain 21 points wins the game.

Throw softball. Six to eight players may be assigned to a team. The object of the garne is to run the bases without being put out. Instead of batting the ball, the batter catches the pitch and throws it into the field. The game is then played as regulation softball. If the batter drops the ball in the strike zone, throws a foul ball or misses a base, the player is out.

Hit pin softball. Two teams may play, each consisting of eight to ten players. Using a diamond with 45 foot baselines, an In than ' club is placed at the outside corner of each base and in the middle of' home plate. Fielders scatter with a pitcher, catcher, and baseman at each base. After batting the ball into fair territory, the runner attempts to circle the outside of the bases and touch, home plate before the fielders can throw the ball to first, second, third, and home consecutively. The baseman at each base must catch the bail arid knock over the pin with a foot before throwing to the next base, If all four pins are knocked over before the runner gets home, an out is scored. One point is awarded for each home run.

Around the horn. Eight players per team may participate, Two fielders are stationed at each of the diamond's four bases. The ball starts at home with the catcher. As the runner runs from home to round the bases, the catcher throws to first. Tile base must be tagged with a foot by the first baseman and then relayed to second. At each base the same procedure must be followed until the ball is returned to the catcher. The fielders must throw the ball around the bases twice before the runner tags all bases and reaches home. One fielder at the base catches the first throw and the second fielder catches the second round throw. One point is scored for each successful run. Teams change sides after all members have a turn, or after a designated number of outs.

One old cat. Three or more players may participate in this game. The batter attempts to stay at bat as long as possible. The batter must hit the ball and run to first base and back to home plate before the ball is returned to the catcher. If the batter scores five runs before being put out, the players rotate: batter to right field, right to center field, center to left field, left to third base, third to shortstop, short to second base, second to first base, first to pitcher, pitcher to catcher, and catcher to batter. Catching a fly ball automatically puts a fielder up to bat. The batter goes to the end of the rotation and other players move up to fill the vacant position of the fielder who caught the ball., The player with the most runs wins the game.

Peggy. Unlimited fielders scatter in an open playing area A batter, catcher, and pitcher assume regular positions. The object of the game is to become the batter. This goal may be attained by any one of the several means:

1. Catching a batted fly ball
2. Catching a batted ball that has taken only one bounce
3. Catching five batted ground balls (without fumbling) hit by one batter. Ground balls are not
4. The catcher catches two balls that have been swung at and missed by the same batter.

Team pepper. (Develops batting, pitching, and fielding skills) With eight to ten players on a team each team forms a circle with one batter in the center. Each player around the circle takes a turn at pitching a ball to the center batter who place hits the ball to the player on the pitcher's left. If the batter misses the ball, it must be returned to the player who pitched the ball. If the fielder misses the ball, the batter must rehit the ball to that fielder before continuing. A round consists of everyone on the team having an opportunity to bat. The team that finishes the round first is declared the winner.

Due to the limited time of class sessions, the increasing coeducational nature of physical education and recreational play, and the skill differences among the players, adaptations in the official game may be desirable. Two popular examples of modified games, suitable for all levels of play, are one-pitch softball and co-recreational softball, A third game, sixteen-inch softball requires greater strength in the execution of throwing and batting skills.

One-pitch softball. To speed up play one-pitch softball is recommended. The pitcher is furnished by the batting team. A member of the fielding team is positioned in the proximity of the pitcher's

1. Since the batter and pitcher are teammates, the pitcher will attempt to throw good pitches and
2. The batter is out if the ball is missed, hit foul, or if a swing is not attempted.
3. Stealing and bunting are prohibited.
4. Players are expected to run on and off the field.
5. For any delay by the batting team in getting the batter or pitcher ready, an out is declared.
6. As soon as the pitcher and batter are in place, the ball may be pitched. This encourages the fielders to assume their positions readily.

7. Official softball rules are applied in all other situations,

Co-recreational softball. Co-recreational softball is a popular game in which men and women play on the same team competitively. Rule modifications are made primarily to equalize any skill differences that may be found between men and women players. The number and degree of modifications made depend on factors such as skill, age of the players, and purpose of the game. In situations where the skill level is high, the only changes may be in the determination of the number of men and women on a team and allowing pinch hitters to be used only for the same sex. In situations where the skill level between men and women needs to be equalized, more extreme modifications may be desirable. Examples of modifications that may be appropriate include the following:

1. Pitching a 16-inch softball to men batters and a regulation softball to women batters.
2. Men batters must bat from the non-preferred side of the plate, eg., men that customarily hit from the right-hand side of the plate must hit from the left-hand side.
3. Male and female batters must be alternated in the batting order.
4. Sliding is not permitted.

Sixteen-inch softball. By replacing the standard 12-inch ball with an official 16-inch ball the batter is given a larger target. Less playing space is needed, and fielders are assisted by a decrease in the flight and speed of the larger ball. Rules are similar to the 12-inch slow-pitch rules with a few exceptions:

1. The baselines are reduced to 55 feet (18.15 meters) for men and 50 feet (16.5 meters) for women, if desired.
2. The pitching plate is 3 8 feet (12.54 meters) from home plate.
3. The pitcher may use two hesitation pitches prior to the mandatory pitch.
4. The pitcher's foot may be in contact with the pitcher's plate when a pickoff is attempted.
5. A strike is called for each foul tip.
6. The batter is out on a third strike, including an uncaught foul ball.
7. A player may lead off from base with a risk of being picked off, but may not advance on a resultant overthrow.
8. The ball is in play on a ball or strike, including the third strike.

Game play for beginners

In teaching softball to children and unskilled players, it may be desirable to modify the official rules for purposes of player enjoyment. The following rule adaptations are suggested for consideration in teaching a beginning softball class:'

1. Softer balls may be substituted for the regulation 12-inch softball. In addition, slower flight balls and super-soft softballs allow defensive players additional time to make plays and deters player

fear of injury when catching a hard bit ball. A 16-inch ball may be used, when space is limited.

2. The diamond dimensions may be altered to include:
   a. Lengthening the baselines from 45 to 55 feet, which allows an unskilled defensive player more time to successfully complete outs.
   b. Increasing the distance between home plate and the pitcher's plate for safety reasons and to increase the pitcher's potential as a fielder.
3. Only slow-pitch pitching is allowed,
4. Players may steal second or third, but to avoid any collisions or dangerous plays at the plate, they may not steal home.
5. Despite the location of a ball in foul territory, only one base on an overthrow is allowed.
6. Regardless of how the catcher handles the pitch, a batter is declared automatically out on the third strike.
7. The infield fly rule is optional.

9

COMPETETIVE SOFTBALL

This chapter discusses the responsibilities of a softball coach—administrative duties, organization techniques—and presents suggestions for practice and games to assist the beginning coach.

Scheduling. Ideally, the scheduling of interscholastic games should be initiated at the completion of the previous season and finalized well in advance of the first game. This allows time for transportation, budgetary, and facility arrangements. Consideration should be given to scheduling easier competition for games early in the season, thus allowing the team sufficient time to prepare for major competition. In recreation leagues, a director prepares and issues the schedule to all teams. However, the coach may schedule additional invitational tournaments or practice games.

Contracting. Contracts should be signed by the teams involved to bind the agreement.

Obtaining travel permits. Travel permits should be signed by the parents or guardians of all minors for away and overnight trips. Although such permits do not relegate the coach's or school's liability, obtaining parental consent is a courtesy that promotes a cooperative effort between the parents and coaches.

Budgeting. Each spring, interscholastic budgetary requests must be submitted by the coach to the athletic director. Requests should be based upon program needs, which are assessed through an accurate inventory, a tentative schedule of games, and budgetary expenditures during the past five years. The coach must consider the expenses which will be incurred for transportation, officials, uniforms, laundry service, equipment and supplies, maintenance, lights, and field rental and improvements. Estimated receipts may include fund raising activities, donations, admission fees, and school allocations.

Procuring officials. Quality officials may be available through the local officiating board, or will be assigned by the league or conference director.

Transporting players. For safety and liability purposes, interscholastic players should be transported by a school bus or van, as opposed to personal cars. It is strongly recommended and sometimes required that the driver possesses a certified chauffeur's license.

Ordering. Once the budget has been approved, equipment and uniforms should be ordered promptly. Orders with specifications that deviate from standard, in-stock items require additional time for manufacturing.

Selecting a team. Although budgetary and philosophical considerations affect the coach's decision regarding the number of players on the team, it is important to have several utility players. Ideally, each utility player can serve as a back up for more than one position. For competitive fast-pitch play, it is desirable to have three pitchers and three catchers due to the strenuous nature and importance of these positions. Slow-pitch play may require fewer back ups in these positions. In selecting players certain personal qualities in athletes are desirable, such as self-discipline on and off the field, the motivation to excel, and a proper competitive attitude. The team's probability of success may be enhanced by the selection of players who are team-oriented, unselfish, supportive, and respectful of others.

Conducting tryouts. A one to two-week period for tryouts will allow the coach sufficient time to assess each Player's potential. Former varsity players should be expected to try out with other candidates. No player should be guaranteed a position on the squad without meeting the established criteria for that particular season. Running, stretching exercises, ball handling warm-ups, infield and outfield drills, batting practice, baserunning techniques, and game play should be integrated in the tryout sessions.

Meeting with the team. At the initial team meeting the coach, either directly or indirectly, shares the staffs coaching philosophy with the players. In turn, players may be requested to reflect on their personal team goals and expectations for the season. Players should be encouraged to share their ideas and maintain an open line of communication as a team, but must realize that all final decisions rest with the coach. The humanistic coach knows that players who strive for and attain realistic goals may have improved self-images, self-awareness, and a better team concept.

The coach must be certain every player is knowledgeable of the coach's expectations for the season. Training rules and eligibility regulations must be understood by all concerned, including the parents. Policy information should be disseminated to guardians of all players through a letter from the coach or parental attendance at team meetings. Players must be knowledgeable of proper diet, sleeping, and study habits. Frequently, a dedicated athlete will become so involved in athletics that academics are no longer valued. It is the coach's responsibility to integrate athletics with the total school experience.

Building good public relations. Sound public relations can result in good community support for the team. Once the team is selected, the coach should prepare information for the media on returning players, new prospects, and the season's schedule. Sportscasters and sportswriters of local and school newspapers may be contacted for possible coverage during the season.

On away games, the scorekeeper or manager can be delegated, immediately after each game, the responsibility of furnishing game results to newspapers and radio and television stations. In addition, local newspapers frequently run a daily section on high school sports, including an Athlete of the Week article. Outstanding athletes or performances should be brought to the sportswriters' attention.

The coach may arouse community interest through talks to civic groups, by organizing team projects which serve the community, and by initiating an active softball booster organization.

Responsibilities

Mentally preparing the team

During the competitive season the coach is faced, with the task of mentally preparing the team for each game.

Generally, however, there is no problem in generating enthusiasm at the beginning of the season or against rival schools. In mentally preparing a team, the coach must stress the team concept, the importance of each game, the value of giving 100 percent effort at all times, and proper respect for the abilities of opponents and teammates.

A team may meet prior to a game and share realistic team objectives and strategies for the contest. Caution must be taken not to assert undue pressure on the players to win, through negative reinforcement.

At practice on the day following a game, techniques or strategies which were faulty should be analyzed and improved upon. Viewing films of the game may be extremely helpful in this analysis. Once the highlights and mistakes of the previous game have been discussed, it becomes past history and every team member should concentrate on preparing for the next game.

Conducting practice sessions

During the practice sessions, the coach must analyze player skills, and offer kinesthetic explanations for faulty performance in terms understood by the players. The key to successful coaching is the ability to capitalize on the strengths and compensate for the weaknesses of individual players. Once the coach analyzes each player's performance., the necessary adjustments may be made for competitive play. For example, a player with inadequate batting skills but strong fielding ability may play a key position on the field yet bat in a less demanding position in the batting order. Conversely, a strong batter but poor fielder could be a designated bitter.

Daily practice sessions should be mentally and physically challenging and include calisthenics, warm-ups, infield and outfield practice, baserunning, and batting practice. Specific days should be devoted to rundowns, relays and cutoffs, squeeze plays, and other offensive and defensive strategies. Drills need to be as game-like as possible. Once the season begins, a team should spend little time scrimmaging.

Each practice should start with stretching exercises. When properly warmed up, an athlete may be less likely to sustain strains and sprains in the muscles, tendons, and ligaments. The range of motion in the joints is increased, and coordination is improved. After players have warmed up sufficiently, they will need to go through a series of drills to warm up their throwing arms. The practice can then continue with drills necessary to prepare the team for the next game.

The sample practice schedule gives a basic plan for organizing practices. Drills should progress from simple to complex. It is important to vary practices to keep players alert mentally and challenged physically.

A practice schedule, similar to the one cited, may keep the team active for approximately two hours. Practices of longer duration may be ineffective.

Staffing

An integral part of a softball team is the coach's supporting staff. Few schools hire an assistant coach. However, knowledgeable parents, community members, former players, or university students may be interested in donating time in order to gain coaching experience.

A qualified scorekeeper and team statistician are necessary to keep accurate records. Such records assist the coach in planning practices and in strategically playing the team members. Additionally, the coach who has accurate statistics on players can assist the scouted athletes desiring college scholarships.

The team manager is responsible for securing eligibility slips, caring for equipment, and having the field lined off before each game. The manager also attends all practices and games, and assists in any capacity deemed necessary by the coach.

It is not always possible for a team physician to be at every game. However, a physician should be on-call in the event of a serious injury. It is strongly recommended that a trainer attend all practices and games. In addition, students who have successfully completed a first aid course, or preferably the Cramer Student Trainer Course, may be valuable assets to any athletic team and athletic trainer.

Conducting warm-ups

Proper selection and use of warm-up drills is very important to effective team play. Warm-up drills may have a psychological as well as physiological effect on a team. Players often need the opportunity to warm up muscles and become conditioned to the field environment. In addition, a well planned and executed drill can boost a team's confidence and offer an impressive display of player Skill and team organization. The pre-game and pre-inning warm-ups in this chapter may be used as presented, or may be modified for use with different skill levels.

Pre-game batting practice

Approximately one hour prior to game time, each player should be allowed ten to 15 warm-up hits. When the field must be shared, the home team practices in left field and the visitors in right field, with batters assuming positions along the third and first base fines respectively. Fielders assume scattered positions in the field and rotate clockwise to become the batter. To expedite the process, the right fielder should rotate to an on-deck position. During the first few hits the batter should be concerned primarily with making contact and executing a fluid swing. Subsequent attempts should receive place hitting emphasis.

Pre-game infield warm-up

The coach fungo hits to infielders in the following suggested sequence:

1. A ground ball is hit to third base. The third baseman throws to first base. The first baseman returns the bail to third. The ball is then thrown from second, to first, and to the catcher.

2. A ground ball is hit to the shortstop. The shortstop throws the ball to first. The first baseman throws to the shortstop covering second. The ball is thrown from second to first to the catcher.

3. A ground ball is hit to the second baseman. The throw is made to first base. The first baseman returns the ball to the second baseman covering the base. The ball is thrown, from second to first to the catcher.

4. A ground ball is hit to the first baseman, who tosses to the second baseman covering first. The

ball is thrown to the catcher and returned to the first baseman covering the bag. The first baseman throws to the catcher.

5. A ball is bunted a' short distance in front of home plate. The catcher fields the bail and throws to first. The first baseman throws back to the catcher covering home.
6. A ground ball is hit to each infielder who tags or throws to the closest bag and completes one of the following double plays: second to first, third to second, first to third, home to second.

Pre-game oufield warm-up

While infielders are warming up the following outfield drill should be conducted. A batter standing on the outfield foul line fungo hits balls to players in a shuttle-line formation. In turn, each player catches the ball and returns it to a catcher beside the fungo batter and takes a position at the end of the line.

Toward the end of the infielder's practice time, the starting outfielders take their respective positions on the field and participate in the following drills which complete their warm-up.

1. A fly ball is hit respectively to the left, center, and right fielders. The fielders return the ball to the catcher on the first bounce.
2. A fly ball is hit to left and center fielders. The fielders throw to second baseman covering second. The ball is relayed from second, to first, to the catcher.

A ground ball is hit to each infielder. The infielder throws the ball to the catcher and charges toward home. The catcher then rolls a second ball back to the charging player. The second ball fielded is tossed easily to the catcher, and the player continues off the field. Outfielders are hit short balls. Each fielder catches the ball, throws it to the catcher and runs off the field.

Pre-inning warm-up

As the pitcher warms up by pitching the legal number of pitches to the catcher, the first baseman throws ground balls to the third baseman, shortstop, and second baseman. Each infielder fields the ball and throws to the first baseman. The outfielders take their positions in the field and practice throwing in relay formation to one another. The left fielder throws to the short fielder, the short fielder to the center fielder, the center fielder to the right fielder. The process is then repeated in reverse order. If the defensive team's bench is on the first base line the right fielder assumes responsibility for starting the warm-up. An alternative Slow-pitch warm-up involves the left fielder and center field throwing to each other, while the short fielder and right fielder do likewise.

Determining the lineup

Prior to the game the coach should develop the lineup based upon players' performances and attitudes in recent games and practices. There are varying theories on whether strong hitters should be staggered in the lineup or stacked at the beginning. A coach must be aware that players at the beginning of the lineup have more times at bat. Standard procedure dictates the first batter should be a good hitter and baserunner. In addition, this batter should be able to judge balls and strikes accurately and get on base. Ideally, the second batter would be left-handed and capable of hitting behind a runner. The team's best hitters will be third and fifth in the order, with a long-ball hitter batting fourth.

The next best hitter bats sixth. The seventh hitter is frequently the second-best leadoff batter, capable of getting on base. The last few batters should have sufficient bunting ability to advance any runners. Coaches should be familiar with the current designated hitter and reentry rules when determining the strongest possible lineup.

Bass coaching

Offensive signals need to be developed by the batter and coach. Players should give a signal as they approach the plate to indicate to the coach: "I'm ready to watch the ball meet the bat." The coach should have signals to indicate such cues as: "Take it," "Go left," "Go right," "Up the middle," Hit away."

Players must have faith in the base coaches' judgments and obey signals without hesitation. As soon as the ball is hit, the, batter becomes a baserunner, and should be looking directly at the first base coach.

The first base coach will let the runner know whether to overrun the bag or make a turn toward second.

As a runner nears second base, eye contact must be made with the third base coach. The coach will indicate whether to slide, hold up, or continue running to third. When the runner comes toward third, the coach will again indicate what the baserunner should do. Throughout the game, and at its conclusion, coaches and players should display good sportsmanship. Win or lose, a congratulatory gesture in the form of a hand-shaking line communicates the players appreciation for the opposing team.

10

RULES AND REGULATIONS

The Official Softball

a. Shall be a regular, smooth-seamed, concealed stitched or flat surfaced ball.

b. Shall have center core made of either No.1 quality, long fibre kapok, a mixture of cork and rubber, a polyurethane mixture, or other materials approved by the individual governing bodies of the international softball federation.

c. May be hand or machine wound, with a fine quality twisted yarn, and covered with latex or rubber cement.

d. Shall have a cover cemented to the ball by application of cement to the under-side of the cover, and swen with waxed thread of cotton or linen, or shall have a molded cover bonded to the core with an authentic facsimile of stitching as approved by the individual governing bodies of the international softball federation.

e. Shall have a cover of the finest quality No.1 chrome tanned horsehide or cowhide, made of synthetic material, or made of other materials approved by the individual governing bodies of the international soft-ball federation.

f. Softballs used in championship play must meet the standards set by the SBAI playing rules.

4. The home plate shall be made of rubber or other suitable materials. It shall be a five-sided figure, 45.0cm (17 in.) wide, across the edge facing the pitcher. The sides shall be parallel to the inside lines of the batter's box and shall be 20.0cm (8-¼ in.) long. The sides of the point facing the catcher shall be 30.0cm, (12 in.) long.

5. The pitcher's plate shall be of rubber, 60cm (24 in) long and 15 cm (6 in) wide. The top of the plate shall be level with the ground. The front line of the plate shall be the following distance from the outside corner of home plate: Male 14.0 m (46 ft); Female 12.0m (40 ft).

6. The bases, other than home plate, shall be 40.0 cm (15 in.) square and shall be made of canvasor other suitable material and not more than 13 cm, (5in) in thickness. The bases should be securely fastened in position.

7. Gloves may be worn by any player, but mitts may be used only by the catcher and first baseman. No top lacing, webbing or other device between the thumb and body of the glove or mitt worn by a first baseman or other fielder shall be more than 13.0 cm (5 in) in length. The pitcher's glove shall be of one solid colour, other than white or grey, multicolour gloves are acceptable for all other players, Gloves with white or grey circles on the outside, giving the appearance of a ball, are illegal for all players.

8. Shoes must be worn by all players. A shoe shall be

considered official if it is made with either canvas or leather uppers or similar materials. The soles may be either smooth or with soft or hard rubber cleats. Ordinary metal sole and heel plates may be used if the spikes on the plate do not extend more than 2.0 cm (¾ in.) from the sole of heel of the shoe. Shoes with rounded metal spikes are illegal.

No hard plastic nylon or polyurethane spikes similar to a metal sole and heal plate, or shoes with detachable cleats that could live an exposed fastener, are allowed in any division at any level of play.

A bat is altered when the physical structure of a legal bat has been changed. Examples of altering a bat are replacing the handle of a metal bat with a wooden or other type handle, inserting material inside the bat, applying excessive tape (more than two layers) to the bat grip, or painting a bat at the top or bottom for other than identification purposes. Replacing the grip with another legal grip is not considered altering the bat. A 'flare or cone' grip attached to the bat is an altered bat.

A live or dead ball appeal play is a play upon which an umpire cannot make a decision until requested by a manager, coach or player of the defensive team. The appeal must be made before the next pitch, legal or illegal. If the appeal is made at the end of an inning or at the end of a game, said appeal will not be accepted if all the players of the defensive team have abandoned fair territory.

A base on balls permits a batter to gain first base without liability to be put out and is warded to a batter by the umpire when four pitches are judged to be balls. A base path is an imaginary line 1.0 m (3 ft) to either side of a direct line between the bases. A baserunner is a player of the team at bat who has finished his/her turn at bat, reached first base, and has not yet been put cut.

A batted ball is any ball that hits the bat or is hit by the bat and which lands either in fair or foul territory. No intention to hit the ball is necessary. The batter's box is the are to which the batter is restricted while in position with the intention of helping his/her team to obtain runs. The lines are considered inside the batter's box. Prior to pitch the batter must have both feet entirely within the lines of the batter's box. A batter-baserunner is a player who has finished his/her turn at bat but has not yet been put out or touched first base. The batting order is the official listing of offensive players in the order in which members of that team must come to bat. When the lineup card is submitted, it shall also include the players' positions. A blocked ball is a batted or thrown ball that is touched, stopped, or handled by a person not engaged in the game, or which touches any object which is not part of the official equipment or official playing area. Effect. The ball is dead. For offensive equipment causing a blocked ball (and creating interference), the player being played on is out. If no apparent play if obvious no runner will be called out but all runners will return to the last base touched at the time of the dead ball declaration.

A bunt is a legally tapped ball not swung at, but intentionally met with the bat and tapped slowly within the infield. A catch is a legally caught ball which occurs when the fielder catches a batted or thrown ball with his/her hands or glove. If the ball is merely held in the fielder's arms or prevented from dropping to the ground by some part of the fielder's body or clothing, the catch is not completed until the ball is in the grasp of the fielder's hands or glove. It is not a catch if a fielder, immediately after he/she contacts the ball, collides with another player or wall or falls to the ground, and drops the ball as a result of the collision or falling to the ground. In establishing a valid catch, the fielder shall hold the ball long enough to prove he/she has complete control of the ball and that his/her release of the ball is voluntary and intentional. If a player drops the ball while in the act of throwing it, it is a valid catch.

The catcher's box is that area within which the catcher must stand while and until the pitched ball is released. The lines are to be considered within the catcher's box. A charged conference takes place when:

a. The defensive team requests a suspension of play for any reason and a representative (not in the field) of the defensive team enters the playing field and gives the umpire cause to believe that he/she has delivered a message (by any means) to the pitcher. When the representative from the dugout enters the filed and removes the pitcher, from the pitching position, it is not a charged conference for the new pitcher, but is a charged conference for the pitcher removed from the pitching position. It is not a charged conference for the defense if they confer during a charged offensive, conference as long as they are ready to play ball when the offense is ready.

b. The offensive team requests a suspension of play to

allow the manager or other team representatives to confer with the batter or base-runner. It is not a charged conference when a pitcher is putting on a warm-up jacket while on base, or if the offense confers while the defensive team is in conference, as long as the offense is ready to play when the defense is ready.

A coach is a member of the team at bat who takes his/her place within the coach's lines on the field to direct the players of his/her team in running the bases. Two coaches are allowed. One coach can have in his/her possession in the coach's box, a scorebook, pen or pencil, and an indicator, which shall be used for scorebook, pen or pencil, and an indicator, which shall be used for used for scorekeeping or record keeping purposes only.

The ball is not in play and is not considered in play again until the pitcher has the ball in his/her possession and is within 2.5m (8 ft.) of the pitcher's plate and the plate umpire has called `Play Ball'. The defensive team is the team in the field. A dislodged base is a base dislodged from its proper position. A double play is a play by the defense in which two offensive players are legally put out as a result of continuous action.

A fair ball is a batted ball that:

a. Settles or is touched on fair territory between home and first base or between home and third base.

b. Bounds past first or third base on or over fair territory.

c. Touches first, second or third base.

d. While on or over fair territory touches the person or clothing of an umpire or player.

e. First fall on fair territory beyond first and third base.

f. While over fair territory, passes out of the playing field beyond the outfield fence.

Fair territory is that part of the playing field within and including the first and third base foul lines from home base to the bottom of the extreme playing field fence and perpendicularly upwards.

A fielder is any player of the team in the field.

A fly ball is any ball batted into the air.

A force-out is an out which can be made only when a baserunner loses the right to the base which he/she is occupying because the batter becomes a baserunner, and before the batter or a succeeding baserunner has been put out.

A foul ball is a batted ball that:

a. Settles on foul territory between home and first base, or between home and third base.

b. Bounds past first or third base on or over foul territory.

c. First touches on foul territory beyond first of third base.

d. While on or over foul territory, touches the person or clothing of an umpire or players, or any object foreign to the natural ground.

e. Touches batter or bat in batter's hand while within the batter's box.

A foul tip is a batted ball which:

a. Goes directly from the bat to the catcher's hands;

b. Goes not higher than the batter's head; and

c. Is legally caught by the catcher.

A helmet may or may not have ear flaps and shall be the type which has safety features equal to or greater than those provided by the full plastic cap with padding on the inside. A liner covering the ears only, does not meet the rule specifications.

The home team is the team on whose grounds the game is played, or if the game is played on neutral ground, the home team shall be designated by mutual agreement or by a flip of a coin.

An illegally batted ball occurs when:

a. A batter hits a ball fair or foul while his/her entire foot is completely out of the box, on the ground, when he/she hits the ball.

b. Any part of the batter's foot is touching home plate when he/she hits the ball.

c. The batter hits the ball with an illegal bat.

An illegally caught ball occurs when a fielder catches a batted or thrown ball with his/her cap, mask, glove, or any part of his/her uniform while it is detached from its proper place. In flight describes any batted, thrown or pitched ball which has not yet touched the ground or some object other than a fielder.

In jeopardy is a team indicating that the ball is in play and an offensive player may be put out. The infield is that portion of the field in fair territory which includes areas normally covered by infielders. An in field fly is a fair fly ball (not including a line drive or an attempted bunt) which can be caught by an infielder with ordinary effort, when first and second, or first, second and third bases are occupied, before two are out. The pitcher, catcher and any outfielder who positions himself/herself in the in filed on the play shall be considered infielders for the purpose of this rule.

An inning is that portion of a game within which the teams alternate on offense and defense and in which there are three outs for each team. A new inning begins immediately after the final out of the previous inning. Interference is the act of an offensive player or team member which impedes, hinders or confuses a defensive player attempting to execute a play.

A legal touch occurs when a runner or batter-baserunner who is not touching a base is touched by the ball while it is securely held in the fielder's hand. The ball is not considered as having been securely held if it is juggled or dropped by the fielder after having touched the runner unless the runner deliberately knocks the ball from the hand of the fielder. It is sufficient for the runner to be touched with the hand or glove in which the ball is held.

A legally caught ball occurs when a fielder catches a batted or thrown ball provided it is not caught in the fielder's hat, cap, mask, protector, pocket, or other part of his/her uniform. It must be caught and firmly held with hand or hands.

A line drive is a fly ball that is batted sharply and directly into the playing field.

Obstruction is the act of:

a. A defensive player or team member which hinders or prevents a batter from striking or hitting a pitched ball.

b. A fielder. While not in possession of the ball, or not in the act of fielding a batted ball, which impedes the progress of a baserunner who is legally running bases.

The outfield is that portion of the field which is outside the diamond formed by the baselines or the area not normally covered by an infielder and within the foul lines beyond first and third bases, and boundaries of the grounds.

An overslide is the act of an offensive player when as a baserunner he overslides a base he/she is attempting to reach, it is usually caused when his/her momentum causes him/her to lose contact with the base which then causes him/her to be in jeopardy. The batter-runner overslide first base without being in jeopardy if he/she immediately returns to that base.

An overthrow is a play in which a ball is thrown from one fielder to another to retire a runner who has not reached or is off base, and which goes into foul territory beyond the boundary lines of the playing field. A passed ball is a legally delivered ball that should have been held or controlled by the catcher with ordinary effort.

The act performed by the pitcher in throwing the ball to the batter. The pivot foot is that foot which the pitcher pushes off the pitcher's plate.

Play Ball is the term used by the plate umpire to indicate that play shall begin or be resumed when the pitcher has the ball in his/her possession and is within 2.5 m (8 ft.) of the pitcher's plate. All defensive players, except the catcher, who must be in the catcher's box, must be in fair territory to put the ball in play.

A quick return pitch is one made by the pitcher with the obvious attempt to catch the batter off balance. This would be before the batter takes his/her desired position in the batter's box or while he/she is still off balance as a result of the previous pitch.

A sacrifice fly is scored when, with less than two outs, the batter scores a runner with a fly ball which is caught. The players listed on the official lineup given to the Umpire-in-Chief and/or the plate umpire. Stealing is the act of a baserunner attempting to advance during a pitch to the batter.

The strike zone is that space over any part of home plate which is between the batter's arm pits and the top of his/her knees when the batter assumes his/her natural batting stance. The act performed by a fielder when throwing the ball to another fielder. Time out is the term used by the umpire to order the suspension of play. A triple play is a continuous action play by the defense in which three offensive players are put out.

A turn at bat begins when a player first enters the batter's box and continues until he/she is put out or becomes a baserunner.

A wild pitch is a legally delivered ball so high, so low, or so wide of the plate that the catcher cannot or does not stop and control it with ordinary efforts

The Playing Field

The playing field is the area within which the ball may be legally played and fielded. The playing field shall have a clear and unobstructed area within the minimum radius of 60.0m (200 ft) for female and 70.00m (225 ft) for male from home plate between the foul lines. Outside the foul lines and between home plate and backstop there shall be an unobstructed area of not less than 8.0 m (25 ft) nor more than 9.0m (30 ft.) in width.

Ground or special rules establishing the limits of the playing field may be agreed upon by leagues or opposing teams whenever backstops, fences, stands, vehicles, spectators, or other obstructions are within the prescribed area. Any obstruction on fair territory less than 60.0m (200 ft.) for female and 70.0m (225 ft.) for male from home plate should be clearly marked for the umpire's information.

To determine the position of home plate, draw a line in the direction it is desired to lay the diamond. Drive a stake at the corner of home plate nearest the catcher. Fasten a cord to this stake and tie knots or otherwise mark the cord at.

Place the cord market-this will be the front line at the middle of the pitcher's plate. Along the same line, drive a stake at the 25.86 m (84 ft.10 in.) marker this will be the center of second base.

Place the 36.6 m (120 ft.) marker at the center of second base and, taking hold of the cord at the 18.3 m (60 ft.) marker, walk to the right of the direction line until the cord is taut and drive a stake at the 18.3 m (60 ft.) marker, this will be the outside corner of first base and the cord will now from the lines to first and second bases. Again, holding the cord at the 18.3 m (60 ft.) marker, walk across the field and in like manner, mark the outside corner of third base. Home plate, first and third bases are wholly inside the diamond.

To check the diamond, place the home plate end of the cord at the first base stake and the 36.6 m (120 ft.) marker at third base. The 18.3 m (60 ft.) marker should now check at home plate and second base.

Check all distances with a steel tape whenever possible.

a. The one-meter (3 ft.) Line is drawn parallel to and 1.0 m (3 ft.) from the base line starting at a point halfway between home plate and first base.

b. The batter's on-deck circle, is a 1.5 m (5 ft.) circle, 0.75 m (2.50 Ft.) radius placed adjacent to the end of player's bench or dugout area closest to home plate.

c. The batter's box, one on each side of home plate, shall measure 1.0 (3 ft.) by 2.2 m (7 ft.), The inside lines of the batter's box shall be 15.0 cm (6 in) from home plate. The front line of the box shall be 1.2 m (4 ft) in front of a line drawn through the center of home plate. The lines are considered inside the batter's box.

d. The catcher's box shall be 3.0 m (10 ft.) in length from the rear outside corners of the batter's boxes and shall be 2.5 m (8 ft.) wide.

e. The coach's box is behind a line 5.0 m (15 ft.) long drawn outside the diamond. The line is parallel to and 2.5 m (8 ft.) from the first and third baseline extended from the bases toward home plate.

f. The pitcher's plate shall have a 5.0 m. (16 ft.) circle drawn from the pitcher's plate, 2.5 m (8 ft.) in radius.

Equipment

1. The official bat:

a. Shall be made of one piece of hardwood, or formed from a block of wood consisting of two or more pieces of wood bonded together with an adhesive in such a way that the grain direction of all pieces is essentially parallel to the length of the bat.

b. Shall be plastic, bamboo, graphite, metal, magnesium, or any combination of these materials.

c. Can be laminated, but must contain only wood or adhesive and have a clear finish.

d. Shall be round or three sided, and shall be smooth.

e. Shall not be more than 87.0 cm (34 inches) long, nor exceed 1100.0 g (38 ounces) in weight.

f. If round; shall not be more than 6.0 cm (2.25 inches) in diameter at its largest part; and if three sided, shall not exceed 6.0 cm (2.25 inches) on the hitting surface. A tolerance of 0.90mm (91/32 inches) is permitted to allow for expansion on the round bat.

g. If metal, may be angular.

h. Shall not have exposed rivets, Pins, rough or sharp edges, or any form of exterior fastener that would present a hazard. A metal bat shall be free of burrs.

i. If metal, shall not have a wooden handle.

j. Shall have a safety grip of cork, tape (not smooth

plastic tape), or composition material. The safety grip shall not be more than 25.0cm, (10 inches) and shall not extend more than 40.0cm (15 inches) from the small end of the bat. No substance other than resin may be used on the bat grip.

k. If metal, and not made of one piece construction with the barrel end closed, shall have a rubber or vinyl plastic, insert firmly secured at the large end of the bat.

l. Shall have a safety knob of a minimum of 0.6 cm (one-fourth inch) protruding at a 90-degree angle from the handle, it can be molded, lathed welded, or permanently fastened. A "flare or cone" grip attached to the bat will be considered an altered bat.

m. Shall be marked "Official Softball" by the manufacturer. If the words "Official Softball" cannot be read due to wear on the bat, the bat should be declared legal if it is legal in all other aspects.

2. *Warm-up bats*

a. The on-deck batter may loosen up with two official softball bats, one approved warm-up bat, or a combination not to exceed two.

b. The warm-up bat must be of one-piece construction and must have a safety grip. It must be marked "warm-up" in 3.0 cm (1.25 inches) letters on the barrel end.

The barrel end must be in excess of 6.0 cm (2-¼ inches).

c. Nothing may be attached to a bat such as a donut, fan etc., when loosening up.

Penalty: When using other than a legal warm-up bat, the illegal equipment must be removed from the game. Continued use after removal, would subject the manager to ejection from the game.

Youth only: No metal cleats or shoes with detachable cleats are allowed in any division at any level of play.

a. Masks: Masks with throat protectors, must be worn by adult catchers. Youth catcher must wear masks, throat protector and helmet An extended wire protection attached to the mask can by worn in lieu of the throat protector.

Body protectors must be worn by female catchers.

10. No equipment shall be left lying on the field, either in fair or foul territory.

11. Uniform. All players on a team shall wear uniforms alike in colour, trim and style.

 a. Ball caps must be alike and are;

  (1) Mandatory for all male players and must by worn properly.

  (2) Caps, visors, and headbands are optional for female players but may not be mixed.

 b. Players may wear a uniform, solid coloured undershirt, it is not mandatory that all players wear an undershirt if one player wears one, but those that are worn must be alike, no player may wear ragged, or slit sleeves on exposed undershirts.

c. A number in contrasting colour, at least 15.0 cm (6 in.) high, must be worn on the back of all uniform shirts. No players on the same team may wear identical numbers. The sleeves of the shirt may not be ragged, frayed or slit.

d. Casts, exposed jewellery such as wrist watches, bracelets, large or loop type earrings and neck chains; or other items judged dangerous by the umpire may not be worn during the game.

e. Helmets are mandatory for batters baserunners and catchers, other than catchers. Helmets may not be worm by any other defensive player except for medical reasons.

Players and substitutes

A team shall consist of;

— 9 players

— With a Designated Hitter-10 players

— Male rosters shall include only male players, and female rosters shall include only female players.

Players positions shall be designated as follows:

— Pitcher, catcher, first baseman, second basemen, third baseman, shortstop, left fielder centerfielder and right fielder.

— With a Designated Hitter; Same as in paragraph "A" above plus a "designated hitter".

Designated hitter

— A "Designated Hitter", referred to as a "DH" may be used for any player, provided it is made known prior to the start of the game and his/her name is indicated on the lineup sheet.

— The "DH" must be remain in the same position in the batting order for the entire game.

c. The "DH" may be substituted for at any time either by a pinch-hitter or a pinch-runner who then becomes the "DH". The substitute must be player who has not yet been in the game.

d. The "DH" may not enter the game on defence.

e. The "DH" replaced by pinch-hitter or pinch-runner may not return to the game.

f. The defensive player for whom the "DH" is batting cannot play offense at any time during the game.

g. The player for whom the "DH" is batting must appear in the last place in the batting order given to the umpire-in chief, and/or the plate umpire.

4. Any of the starting players, except "DH", may be withdrawn and reenter once, provided such player occupies the same batting position whenever he/she is in the lineup. Note: The original player and the substitute cannot be in the lineup at the same time.

The penalty for an illegal "DH" entering the game Offensively is as follows:

— If the illegal player is discovered while at bat, he/she is ejected. Any advance of baserunners while the illegal batter is at bat, is legal.

— If the illegal player is discovered after completing his/her turn at bat and prior to the next pitch, the illegal player is ejected and any advance of baserunners as a result of a walk or base hit by the illegal batter, is nullified.

— If the illegal player is discovered after completing his/her turn at bat and after the next pitch, the illegal batter was at bat, is legal.

The penalty for an illegal "DH" entering the game Defensively is as follows;

— If the illegal player is discovered after he/she makes a play and prior to the next pitch, the offensive team has the option of taking the result of the play, or have the last batter go back to bat, assuming balls and strikes prior to the discovery of the illegal player and having all baserunners return to the base they were prior to the play. The illegal player is ejected.

— If the illegal player is detected after a pitch to the next batter, the illegal player is ejected and all plays stand.

The penalty for an illegal re-entry is the ejection of both the manager/coach and the player in violation.

— team must have the required number players present to start or continue a game. No player's name shall be on the starting lineup unless the player is available in the team area in uniform. Requirements are 9 players with a Designated Hitter-10 players.

— A player shall be officially in the game when his/her name has been entered on the official scorestheet or has been announced. A substitute may take the place of a player whose name is in his/her team's batting order. The following regulations govern the substitution of players:

The manager or team representative of the team making the substitution shall immediately notify the plate umpire at the time a substitute enters. Failure to do so would create an illegal substitution with the penalty, immediate removal from the game when the infraction is discovered, and shall not participate again as a player or coach. All play while the illegal substitute is in the game shall stand.

Substitute players will be considered in the game without penalty as follows:

— If a batter, when he/she takes his/her place in the batter's box.

— If a fielder, when he/she takes the place of the fielder substituted for.

— If a runner, when the substitute replaces him/her place on the base he/she is holding.

— If a pitcher, when he/she takes his/her place on the pitcher's plate.

Any player may be removed from the game at any time.

A player removed from the game shall not participate in the game again except as a coach. Exception; The starting lineup may re-enter one time.

Multiple substitutions can be made for the player listed on the starting lineup but no substitute can return to the game after being removed. The starting player who re-enters, and is substituted for a second time, would not be allowed to participate in the game any more. The player who re-enters can play any position on defense, and must remain in the same batting order as a starter.

The Game

The choice of the first or last bat in the inning shall be decided by a toss of a coin. Unless otherwise stated in the rules of the organisation under which the schedule of games is being played.

The fitness of the ground for a game shall be decided solely by the plate umpire.

Regulation game shall consist of seven inning.

— A full seven innings need not be played if the team second at bat scores more, runs in six innings or before the third out in the third out in the last of the seventh inning.

— A game that is tied at the end of seven innings shall be continued by playing additional innings, or until one side has scored more runs than the other at the end of a completed inning, or until the team second at bat has scored more runs in their half of the inning before the third out is made,

— A game called by the umpire shall be regulation if five or more complete innings have been played or if the team second at bat has scored more runs than the other team has scored in five or more innings. The umpire is empowered to call a game at any time because of darkness, rain, fire, panic, or other cause which puts the patrons or players in peril.

— A regulation ties game shall be declared if the score is equal when the game is called at the end of five or more completed innings, or if the team second at bat has equaled the score of the first team at bat in the incomplete innings.

— These provisions do not apply to any acts on the part of players or spectators which might call for forfeiture of the game. The umpire may forfeit the game if attacked physically by any team member or spectator.

A forfeited game shall be declared by the umpire in favour of the team not at fault in the following cases:

— If a team fails to appear on the field, or being on the field, refuses to begin a game for which it is scheduled or assigned at the time scheduled or within a time set for forfeitures by the organization in which the team is playing.

— If, after the game has begun, one side refuses to continue to play, unless the game has been suspended or terminated by the umpire.

— If, after play has been suspended by the umpire one side fails to resume playing within two minutes after the umpire has called "Play ball".

— If a team employs tactics palpably designed to delay or to hasten the game.

— If after a warning by the umpire, any one of the rules of the game is willfully violated.

— If the order for the removal of a player is not obeyed within one minute.

— If, because of the removal of the players from the game by the umpire or for any cause there are less than 9 on either team.

Games that are not considered regulation, or regulation tie games, shall be replayed from the beginning. Original lineups may be changed when the game is replayed. Exception: When a World Championship or continental game or national is suspended by the chief umpire, it shall be resumed at the exact point where the game was suspended.

The winner of the game shall be the team that scores the most runs in a regulation game.

— The score of a called regulation game shall be the score at the end of the last complete inning unless the team second at bat has scored more runs than the first team at bat in the incomplete inning, in this case the score shall be that of the incomplete inning.

— The score of a regulation tie game shall be the tie score when the game was terminated. A regulation tie game shall be replayed from the beginning.

— The score of a forfeited game shall be: 7-0 in favour of the team not at fault.

Tiebreaker: Starting with the top of the tenth inning, and each half inning there after, the offensive team shall begin it's turn at bat, with the player who is scheduled to bat ninth in that respective hale-inning being placed on second base. The player who is running, can be substituted in accordance with the substitution rules.

One run shall be scored each time a baserunner

legally touches first, second, third bases and home plate before the third out of the inning.

A run shall not be scored if the third out of the inning is a result of;

— The batter being put out before legally touching first base.

— A baserunner being forced out due to the batter becoming a baserunner.

— No succeeding runner shall score run when a preceding runner has been declared the third out of an inning.

There shall be only two charged conferences between the manager or other team representative and the batter or baserunner in an inning. Umpires shall not permit any such conferences in excess of two in an inning.

Pitching regulation

The pitcher shall take a position with both feet firmly on the ground and in contact with, but not off the side of, the pitcher's plate.

— The pitcher, while standing on the pitcher's plate, must take the signal from the catcher or look at the catcher. If a signal is taken, it must be taken while pitcher has both feet in contact with the pitcher's plate. The ball must be held in One hand and the hands must be separated.

— Preliminary to pitching, the pitcher must bring his whole body to a full and complete stop facing the batter with his/her shoulders in line with first and third base and with the ball held in both hands in front of the body. This full and complete stop position must be maintained for a minimum of one second and not more than 10 seconds before starting the pitch.

— The pitcher shall not be considered in the pitching position unless the catcher is in position to receive the pitch.

— The pitcher may not take the pitching position on or near the pitcher's plate without having the ball in his/her possession.

The pitch started when one hand is taken off the ball or the pitcher makes any motion that is part of his/her windup. In the act of delivering the ball, the pitcher shall not take more than one step which must be forward, toward the batter, and simultaneous with the delivery of the ball to the batter. The pivot foot may remaining contact or may push off and drag away from the pitching plate prior to the front foot touching the ground, as long as the pivot foot remains in contact with the ground. Pushing off with the pivot foot from a place other than the pitcher's plate is illegal.

A legal delivery shall be a ball which delivered to the batter with an underhanded motion.

— The release of the ball and the follow though of the hand and wrist must be forward, past the straight line of the body.

— The hand shall be below the hip and the wrist not farther from the body than the elbow.

— The pitch is completed with a step toward the batter.

— The catcher must be within the outside lines of the catcher's box when the pitch is released.

— The catcher shall return the ball directly to the pitcher after each pitch, except after a strikeout or putout made by the catcher. The pitcher has 20 seconds to release the next pitch.

The pitcher may use any windup desired, providing:

— He/She does not make any motion to pitch without immediately delivering the ball to the batter.

— He/she does not use a rocker action in which, after having the ball in both hands in pitching position he/she removes one hand from the ball, takes a back-ward and forward swing and returns the ball to both hands in front of the body.

— He/She does not use a windup in which there is a stop or reversal of the forward motion.

— He/She does not make more than one revolution of the arm in the windmill pitch. A pitcher may drop his/her arm to the side and to the rear before starting the windmill motion.

— He/She does not continue to windup after taking the forward step which is simultaneous with the release of the ball.

The pitchers shall not deliberately drop. Roll, or Bounce the ball while in the pitching position in order to prevent the batter from striking it.

The pitcher shall not, at any time during the game, be allowed to use tape or other substances on his pitching hand or fingers nor shall a pitcher use a ball that has a foreign substances on it: Under the supervision and control of the umpire, powdered resin may be used to dry the hands. The pitcher shall not wear a sweatband, bracelet, or similar type item on the writ or forearm of the pitching arm.

No player shall take position in the batter's line of vision or, with deliberate unsportsmanlike intent, act in a manner to distract the batter.

The offender shall be ejected from the game and an illegal pitch shall be declared, even though a pitch may not be released. Any infraction of the sections 1 to 6 is an illegal pitch with the exception of 3e which is covered desperately. The ball is dead. A ball is called on the batter. Baserunners are entitled to advance one base without liability to be put out. If the pitcher completes the delivery of the ball to the batter and the batter hits the ball and reaches first base safety and all baserunners advance at least base one then the play stands and the illegal pitch is nullified. A delayed dead ball will be signified by the umpire by extending his-her left arm horizontally. If there are no baserunner on base and an illegal pitch hits the batter, the batter is awarded first base. An illegal pitch shall be called immediately when it becomes illegal. If called by the plate umpire, it shall be called in a voice so that the catcher and the batter will hear it. The plate umpire will also give the delayed dead ball signal. If called by the base umpire, it shall be called so that the nearest fielder shall hear it. The base umpire shall also give the delayed dead ball signal. Failure of players to hear the call shall not void the call.

At the beginning or each half inning, or when a pitcher relieves another, not more than one minute may be used to deliver not more than five pitches to the catcher or other teammate; Play shall be suspended during this time. For excessive warm-up pitches a pitcher shall be penalized by awarding a ball to the batter for each pitch in excess of five.

The pitcher shall not throw to a base while his/her foot is in contact with the pitcher's plate after he/she has taken the pitcher position.

Illegal pitch, the ball is dead, a ball is called on the batter and all runner advance one base. If the throw from the pitcher's plate is during an appeal play, the appeal is cancelled. The pitcher can remove himself/herself from the pitching position by stepping backwards off the pitcher's plate. Stepping forward or sideways constitutes an illegal pitch.

No pitch shall be declared when:

— The pitcher pitches during the suspension of play.

— The pitcher attempts a quick return of the ball before the batter has taken position or is off balance as a result of a previous pitch.

— The runner is called out for leaving the base too soon.

— The pitcher pitches before a baserunner has retouched his/her base after a foul ball has been declared and the ball is dead.

The ball is dead and all subsequent action on that pitch is cancelled. No player, manager or coach shall call "time" or employ any other word or phrase or commit any act while the ball is alive and in play for the obvious purpose of trying to make the pitcher commit an illegal pitch. No pitch shall be declared and a warning issue to the offending team. A repeat of this type act by the team warned shall result in the offender being removed from the game.

There shall be only one charged conference between the manager or other team representative from the dugout with each and every pitcher in an inning; The second charged conference shall result in the removal of the pitcher from the pitching position for the remainder of the game.

If the ball slips from the pitchers hand during his/her windup or during the backswings, the ball will be in play and the runners may advance at their own risk.

Pitching regulations

All pitching rules are in effect except:

— The pitcher must release the ball on the first forward swing of the pitching arm past the hip.

— The pitcher may not use a windmill or slingshot-type pitch, nor may he make a complete revolution in the delivery. Note: A slingshot-type pitch is defined as turning the body toward first of third base and bending the arm at the elbow during the backswing.

— The pitcher may take the ball behind his back on the backswing.

— The pitcher may drop his arm to the side and to the rear, but the ball may not be seen in the open palm, at the top of the backswing, nor may it be outside the pitcher's wrist at any time on the forward swing.

— The pitcher may not have a stop or reversal of the forward motion of the pitching arm, and he must have a smooth follow-through of the pitching arm on the delivery.

— There is no penalty for touching the hip on the forward· swing.

— The pitcher's palm may be facing up or down on the release of the ball.

— The pitcher may not continue to wind-up after releasing the all, nor may be make any motion to pitch without immediately delivering the ball to the batter.

Batting

The batter shall take his/her position within the lines of the batter's box.

— The batter shall not have his/her entire foot touching the ground completely outside the lines of the batter's box or touching home plate when the ball is hit.

— The batter shall not step directly across in front of the catcher to the other batter's box while the pitcher is in position ready to pitch.

— The batter shall not enter the batter box with an illegal bat.

— The batter shall not enter the batter's box with an altered bat.

The ball is dead, the batter is out, and without warning, the batter is removed from further participation in the game, and baserunner may not advance.

— The batter must take his/her position within 20 seconds after the umpire has called "Play Ball".

The ball is dead. The batter is out. Each player of the side at bat shall become a batter in the order in which his/her name appears on the scoresheet.

— The batting order of each team must be on the score-sheet and must be delivered before the game by the manager or captain to the plate umpire. He/she shall submit it to the inspection of the manger or captain of the opposing team.

— The batting order delivered to the umpire must be followed throughout the game unless a player is substituted for another. When this occurs, the substitute must take the place of the removed player in the batting order.

— The first batter in each inning shall be the batter whose name follows that of the last player who completed a turn at bat in the preceding inning.

Batting out of order is an appeal play which may be made by the manager, coach, or player of the defensive team only.

If the error is discovered while the incorrect batter is at bat, correct batter may take his/her place, assume any balls and strikes, and any runs scored or bases run while the incorrect batter was at bat shall be legal.

If the error is discovered after the incorrect batter has completed his/her turn at bat and before there has been a pitch to another batter, the player who should have batted is out. Any advance or score made because of a ball batted by the improper batter or because of the improper batter's advance to first base on a hit, an error, a base on balls or a hit batter shall be nullified, the next batter is the player whose name follows that of the player called out for failing to bat. If the batter declared out under these circumstances is the third out the correct batter in the next inning shall be the player who would have come to bat had the player been put out by ordinary play.

If the error is discovered after the first pitch to the next batter, the turn at bat of the incorrect batter is legal, all runs scored and bases run are legal, and the next batter in order shall be the one whose name follows that of the incorrect batter. No one is called out for failure to bat. Players who have not bated and who have not been called out have lost their turn at bat until reached again in the regular order.

No baserunner shall be removed from the base he/she is occupying to bat in his/her proper place. He/she merely misses his/her turn at bat with no penalty. The batter following him her in the batting order becomes the legal batter.

— When the third out in an inning is made before the batter has completed his/her turn at bat, he/she shall be the first batter in the next inning and the ball and strike count on him/her shall be cancelled.

The batter shall not hinder the catcher from fielding or throwing the ball by stepping out of the batter's box, or intentionally hinder the catcher while standing within the batter's box.

The ball is dead and baserunners must return to the last base that in the judgement of the umpire, was touched at the time of the interference. The batter is out except.

If a baserunner attempting to steal is put out, the batter is not also out.

With less than two outs and a runner or third base and the batter interferes with a play being made at home plate, the batter is not out because the runner is out.

4. Members of the team at bat shall not interfere with a player attempting to field a foul fly ball.

The ball is dead and the batter is out, and baserunner must return to the base legally held at the time of the pitch.

5. The batter shall not hit a fair ball with the bat a second time in fair territory.

If the batter drops the bat and the ball rolls against the bat in fair territory and in the umpire's judgement, there was no intention to interfere with the course of the ball, the batter is not out and the ball is alive and in play.

The ball is dead, the batter is out, and baserunners may not advance.

6. Strike is called by the umpire:

a. When any part of a legally pitched ball enters the strike zone before touching the ground and at which the batter does not swing.

b. The ball is in play and the baserunners may advance with liability to be put out.

c. For each foul tip held by the catcher.

The ball is in play and baserunners may advance with liability to be put out, The batter is out if it is the third strike.

d. For each foul ball not legally caught on the fly when the batter has less than two strikes.

e. For each pitched ball struck and missed which touches any part of the batter.

f. When any part of the batter's person is hit with his her own batted ball when he/she is in the batter's box and he/she has less than two strikes.

g. When a delivered ball by the pitcher hits the batter while the ball is in the strike zone.

The ball is dead and baserunners must return to their bases without liability to be put out.

7. A ball is called by the umpire;

   a. For each pitched ball which does not enter the strike zone or touches the ground before reaching home plate or touches home plate and which is not struck at by the batter.

      The ball is in play and baserunners are entitled to advance with liability to be put out.

   b. For each illegally pitched ball.

7. The ball is dead and baserunners are entitled to advance one base without liability to be put out.

   c. When the catcher fails, to return the ball directly to the pitcher.

   d. When the pitcher fails to pitch the ball within 20 seconds.

   e. For each excessive warm-up pitch.

      The ball is dead. Baserunners may not advance.

8. A fair ball is a legally batted ball which:

   a. Settles or is touched on fair territory between home and first base or between home and third base.

b. Bounds past first or third base on or over fair territory.

c. Touches first, second or third base.

d. While on or over fair territory touches the person or clothing of an umpire or player.

e. First falls on fair territory beyond first or third base.

f. While over fair territory passes out of the playing field beyond the out field fence.

The ball is in play and baserunners are entitled to advance any number of bases with liability to be put out. The batter becomes a baserunner unless the infield fly rule applies.

g. While on or ever fair ground, lands behind a fence or into a stand a distance of more than 60.0 m (200 ft.) Female 70.0m (225 ft.) Male from home plate. This is considered a home run. If the distance is less than these distances, it is a two-base hit.

h. Hits a foul line pole on the fly. If the ball hits the pole above the fence level. It shall be a home run.

9. A foul ball is a legally batted ball which:

a. Settles on foul territory between home and first base or between home and third base.

b. Bounds past first or third base on or over foul territory.

c. First touches on foul territory beyond first or third base.

d. While on or over foul territory touches the person or clothing of an umpire or player, or any object foreign to the natural ground.

e. Touches batter or bat in batter's hand while within the batter's box.

(1) The ball is dead unless it is a legally caught foul fly. If a foul fly is caught, the batter is out. (2) A strike is called on the batter unless he already had two strikes. (3) Baserunners must return to their bases without liability to be put out unless a foul fly is caught. In this case, the baserunner may advance with liability to be put out after the ball has been touched.

10. A foul tip is batted ball which goes directly from the bat, not higher than the batter's head to catcher's hands and is legally caught by the catcher.

10: A strike is called, the ball remains in play and baserunners may advance with liability to be put out.

11. The batter is out under the following circumstances'

a. When the third strike is struck at and missed and touches any part of the batter's person.

b. When a batter appears in the batter's box with, or is discovered using, an altered bat.

c. When the batter enters the batter's box with an illegal bat or is discovered using an illegal bat.

d. When a fly ball is legally caught.

e. Immediately when he hits an infield fly with baserunners on first and second, or on first, second and third with less than two outs. This is called the infield fly rule.

f. The batter is out if a fielder intentionally drops a fair fly ball (including a line drive) or a bunt which can be caught by an infielder, with ordinary effort, with first, first and second, first and third, or first second and third base occupied with less than two outs.

11f: The ball is dead, and baserunners must return to last base touched at the time of the pitch.

g. The batter-runner is out if a preceding runner who is not yet out, and in the umpire's judgement, intentionally interferes with a fielder who is attempting to catch a thrown ball or to throw a ball in an attempt to complete the play. The runner shall also be called out and interference called.

h. When the third strike is caught by the catcher.

i. When he/she has three strikes if there are less than two outs and first base is occupied.

j. When he/she bunts foul after the second strike. If the ball is caught in the air, it remains alive and in play.

12. The batter or baserunner is not out if a fielder making a play on him/her uses an illegal glove; The manager of the offended team has the option of having the batter bat over and assuming the ball and strike count he/she had prior to the pitch he/she hit, or taking the result of the play.

13. On deck batter

a. The on-deck batter is the offensive player whose name follows the name of the batter in the batting order.

b. The on-deck batter shall take a position within the line of the on-deck circle nearest his/her bench.

c. The on-deck batter may leave the on-deck circle.

(1) When he/she becomes the batter.

(2) To direct baserunners advancing from third to home plate.

d. When the on-deck batter interferes with the defensive player's opportunity to make a play on a runner, the runner closest to home plate at the time of the interference shall be declared out.

Baserunning

The baserunners must touch bases in legal order (i.e. first, second, third, and home plate).

a. When a baserunner must return while the ball is in play, he/she must touch the bases in reverse order.

The ball is in play and baserunners must return with liability to be put out.

b. When a baserunner acquires the right to a base by touching it before being put, out, he/she is entitled to hold the base until he/she has legally touched the next base in order or is forced to vacate if for a succeeding baserunner.

c. When a baserunner dislodges a base from its proper position neither he/she nor succeeding runners in the same series of plays are compelled to follow a base unreasonably out of position.

c. The ball is in play and baserunners may advance with liability to be put out.

d. A baserunners shall not run bases in reverse order either to confuse the fielders or to make a travesty of the game.

e. Two baserunners may not occupy the same base simultaneously.

The runner who first legally occupied the base shall be entitled to it; the other baserunner may be put out by being touched with the ball.

f. Failure of a preceding runner to touch a base, or to leave a base legally on a caught fly ball and who is declared out does not affect the status of a succeeding baserunner who touches bases in proper order, however, if the failure to touch a base in regular order or to leave a base legally on a caught fly ball, is the third out of the inning no succeeding runner may score a run.

g. No runner may return to touch a missed base or one he/she had left illegally, after a following runner has scored.

h. After the ball becomes dead on runner may return to touch a missed base, a base he/she has left after advancing to and touching a base beyond the missed base, or a base he/she left illegally, even after the ball becomes alive.

i. No runner may return to touch a missed base or one he/she had left illegally, once he enters his/her team dugout or bench area.

j. When a walk is issued, all runners must touch all bases in legal order.

k. Bases left too soon on a caught fly ball must be retouched while enroute to awarded bases.

l. Awarded base must also be touched and in proper order.

2. The batter becomes a baserunner;

a. As soon as he/she hits a fair ball.

b. When the catcher fails to catch the third strike before the ball touches the ground when there are less than two out and first base is unoccupied, or anytime there are two outs. This is called the third strike rule.

c. When a fair ball strikes the person or clothing of an umpire on foul ground.

2a. The ball is in play and the batter becomes a batter-baserunner with liability to be put out.

d. When four balls have been called by the umpire.

2d. The ball is in play unless it has been blocked. The batter entitled to one base without liability to be put out.

When the catcher or any other fielder obstructs or prevents the batter from striking at a pitched ball.

2e. The ball is dead. The batter is awarded first base. Baserunners may not advance unless forced.

(1) The umpire shall give a "delayed dead ball signal"

(2) The manager of the batting team has the option of taking the award for "catcher obstruction" as described above, or he/she may take the result of the play.

(3) If the batter hits the ball and reaches first base safely, and if all other runners have advances at least one base on the batted ball, catcher obstruction is cancelled. All action as a result of the batted ball stand. No option is given.

When a fair ball strikes the person or clothing of the umpire or a base runner on fair ground.

(1) If the ball hits umpire or baserunner after passing an infielder other than the pitcher or touched by an infielder including the pitcher, the ball is in play. (2) If the ball hits the umpire or baserunner before passing an infielder, the ball is dead and the batter is entitled to first base without liability to be put out. Baserunners not forced by the batter-baserunner must return.

g. When a pitched ball not struck at, or not called a strike touches any part of the batter's person or clothing while he/she is in the batter's box. It does not matter if the ball strikes the ground before hitting him/her. The batter's hands are not to be considered as part of the bat.

2g: The ball is dead and the batter is entitled to one base without liability to be put out unless he/she made no effort to avoid being hit. In this case, the plate umpire calls either a ball or a strike.

h. When a called illegally pitched ball, not struck at touches any part of the batter's person or clotting while he/she is in the batter's box, and there are no runners on base. It does not matter if the ball strikes the ground before hitting him/her. The batter's hands are not to be considered part of the bat.

2h: The ball is dead and the batter is entitled to one base without liability to be put out unless he/she made no effort to avoid being hit. With runners on base refer to Rule 6 Effect Sec. 1-6 illegal pitch.

3. Baserunners are entitled to advance with liability to be put out under the following circumstance:

a. When a ball leaves the pitcher's hand on a pitch.

b. When the ball is over-thrown in to fair or foul territory and is not blocked,

c. When the ball is bated into fair territory and is not blocked.

d. When legally caught fly ball is first touched.

e. If a fair ball strikes the umpire or a baserunner after having passed an infielder other than the pitcher or having been touched by an fielder including the pitcher the ball shall be considered in play. Also, if a fair ball strikes an umpire on foul ground, the ball shall be in play.

The ball is alive and in play.

4. A player forfeits his/her exemption from liability to get put out;

(a) If while the ball is in play he fails to touch the base to which he was entitled before attempting to make the next base. If the runner put out is batter-baserunner at first or any other baserunner, forced to advance because the batter becomes a baserunner, this out is a force-out.

(b) If after over-running first base, the batter-baserunner attempt to continue to second base.

(c) If after dislodging the base, the batter-baserunner tries to continue to the next base.

5. Baserunners are entitled to advance without liability to be put out:

(a) When forced to vacate a base because the batter was awarded a base on balls.

5.a.The ball remains in play unless it is blocked or obstructed. Baserunner affected is entitled to one base and may advance further at his own risk if the ball is in play.

(b) When a fielder obstructs the baserunner from touching base unless the fielder is trying to field a batted ball or has the ball ready to touch the baserunner.

5.b.All the runners shall be permitted to advance without liability to be put out, to the bases which, in the umpire's judgement the runners would have reached had the fielder not obstructed the runner. The ball is dead.

(c) When a wild pitch or passed ball goes under, over through or lodges in the backstop.

5c.:The ball is dead. All baserunners are awarded one base only. The batter is awarded first base only on the fourth ball.

d. When forced to vacate a base because the batter was awarded a base.

(1) For being hit by a pitched ball.

(2) For being interfered with by the catcher when striking at a pitched ball.

The ball is dead and baserunners may not advance further than the base to which they are entitled.

(3) If, with a runner on third base any trying to score by means of a squeeze play or a steal, the catcher or any other fielder steps on, or in front of home plate without possession of the ball, or touches the batter or his/her bat, the pitcher shall be charged with an illegal pitch, the batter shall be awarded first base on the obstruction, and the ball is dead.

e. When a pitcher makes an illegal pitch.

5e: The ball is dead and baserunner may advance to the base to which they are entitled without liability to be put out.

f. When a fielder contacts or catches a fair batted or thrown ball with his/her cap, mask, glove or any part of his/her uniform while it is detached from its proper place on his/her person.

5f: The baserunners shall be entitled to three bases if a batted ball, or two bases if a thrown ball, and in either case the baserunners may advance further at their own risk. If the illegal catch or touch is made on a fair hit ball which in the opinion of the umpire would have cleared the outfield fence in flight the runner shall be awarded a home run.

g. When the ball is in play and is overthrown (beyond the boundary lines) or is blocked.

5g: All runners will be awarded two bases, and the award will be governed by the position of the runners when the ball left the fielder's hand.

(1) When a fielder loses possession of the ball such as

on an attempted tag, and the ball then enters the dead ball area or becomes blocked, all runners are awarded one base from the last base touched at the time the ball entered the dead ball area or became blocked. If a runner touches the next base and returns to his original base the original base he left is considered the "last base touched" for purposes of an overthrown award.

h. When a fair-batted ball goes over the fence or into the stands, it shall entitle the batter to a home run unless it passes out of the grounds or into a distance less than 60.0m (200 ft) Female, 70.0 m (225 ft) Male from home plate, in which case the batter shall be entitled to two bases only. The batter must touch the base in regular order. The point at which the fence or stand is less than 60.0 m (200 ft) Female, 70.0m (225 ft) Male from home plate shall be plainly indicated for the umpire's guidance.

i. When a fair ball bounds or roll into a stand, over, under or through a fence; bounds out of play unintentionally off a defensive player; or leaves the boundaries of the playing field after touching the ground in fair territory.

The ball, is dead and all baserunners are awarded two bases from time of pitch.

j(1) When a live ball is unintentionally carried by a fielder from playable territory into dead ball territory, the ball become dead. All baserunners are awarded one base from the last base touched at the time he/she enters dead ball territory.

(2) If, in the judgement of the umpire, a fielder intentionally carries a live ball from playable

territory into dead ball territory, the ball becomes dead and all baserunners are awarded two bases from the last base touched at the time he/she entered dead ball territory.

6. A baserunners must return to his/her base under the following circumstances;

a. When a foul ball is illegally caught and is so declared by the umpire.

b. When an illegally batted ball is declared by the umpire.

c. When a batter or baserunner is called out for interference. Other baserunners shall return to the last base which was, in the judgement of the umpire, legally touched by him/her at the time of the interference.

d. When there is interference by the Plate Umpire or his/her clothing with the catcher's attempt to throw.

e. When any part of the batter's person is touched by a pitched ball swung at and missed.

f. When a batter is hit by a pitched ball, unless forced.

g. When a foul ball is not caught.

(1) The ball is dead (2) The baserunners must return to base without liability to be putout except when forced to go to the next base because the batter became a baserunner. (3) No runs shall score unless all bases are occupied. (4) Baserunners need not touch the interviewing bases in returning to base but must return promptly (5) However, they must be allowed sufficient time to return.

h. When a caught fair fly ball (including a line drive) or bunt which can be caught by an infielder with ordinary effort is intentionally dropped with less than two out, with a runner on first base, first and second, first and third, or first, second and third base.

7. Batter-Baserunners are out under the following circumstances;

a. When the catcher drops the third strike and he/she is legally touched with the ball by a fielder before touching first base.

b. When the catcher drops the third strike and the ball is held on first base before the batter-runner reaches first base.

c. When after a fair ball is hit, he/she is legally touched with the ball before he/she touches first base.

d. When after a fair ball is hit, the ball is held by a fielder touching first base with any part of his/her person before the batter-baserunner touches first base.

e. When after a fly ball is hit, the ball is caught by a fielder before it touches the ground or any object other than a fielder.

f. When after a fair ball is hit or a base on ball is issued or when the batter may legally advance to first base on a dropped third strike he/she fails to advance to first base and instead enters his/her team area.

7 The ball is in play and the batter-baserunner is out.

g. When he/she runs outside the 1.0 m (3 ft) line and in the opinion of the umpire interferes with the fielder taking the throw at first base. However, he/she may run outside the 1.0m (3 ft) line to avoid a fielder attempting to field a batted ball.

h. When he interferes with a fielder attempting to field a batted ball or internationally interferes with a thrown ball. If this interference, in the judgement of the umpire, is an obvious attempt to prevent a double play, the baserunner closest to home plate shall also be called out.

i. When a batter-baserunner interferes with a play at home plate in an attempt to prevent an obvious out at the plate. The runner is aiso out.

j. When he/she touches a batted ball over fair ground a second time while his/her bat or any par of his/her body is out of the batter's box in fair territory.

k. When he/she moves back toward home plate to avoid or delay a tag by a fielder

The ball is dead and the batter-baserunner is out. Other baserunners must return to the last base legally touched at the time of or before the illegal action.

The baserunner is out:

a. When a running to any base, he/she runs more than 1.0m (3 ft.) from a direct line between a base and the next one in regular or revers order to avoid being touched by the hand of a fielder.

b. When, while the ball is in play, he/she is legally touched with the ball in the hand of the fielder while not in contact with a base.

c. When on a force-out, a fielder tages him/her with the ball or holds the ball on the base to which the baserunner is forced to advance before the runner reaches the base.

d. When the baserunner fails to return to touch the base he/she previously occupied when play is resumed after suspension of play.

e. When a baserunner physically passes a preceding baserunner before that runner has been put out.

The ball is in play and the baserunner is out.

f. When the baserunner leave his/her base to advance to another base before a caught fly ball has touched a fielder legally touches the baserunner before the baserunner returns to his/her, provided the ball is returned to a fielder and legally held on that base or a fielder legally touches the baserunner before the baserunner returns to his/her base.

g. When the baserunner fails to touch the intervening base or bases in regular or reverse order and the ball is in play and legally held on that base or bases in regular or reverse order and the ball is in play and legally held on that base, or the baserunner is legally touched while off the base he/she missed.

h. When the batter-runner legally over runs first base, attempts to run to second base is legally touched while off base.

i. In running or sliding for home plate, he/she fails to touch home plate, and makes no attempt to return to the plate, when a fielder holds ball in his/her hand while touching home plate, and appeals to the umpire for the decision.

(1) There are appeal plays and the defensive team loses the privilege of putting the baserunner out if the appeal is not made before the next legal or illegal pitch.

(2) The ball is in play and the baserunner is out.

(3) Baserunner may leave their base during live ball appeal plays when the ball leave the radius around the pitcher's plate, or when the ball leaves the pitcher's possession; or when the pitcher makes throwing motion indicating a play or fake throw.

(4) Dead Ball Appeal. Once the ball has been returned to the infield and "time" has been called by the umpire, (or the ball becomes dead) any infielder (including the pitcher or catcher) with or without possession of the ball, may make a verbal appeal on a runner missing a base or leaving a base too soon. The administering umpire should acknowledge the appeal, and then make a decision no play. Baserunners cannot leave their base during this period, as the ball remains dead until the next pitch.

j. When a baserunner is struck with a fair batted ball while off base and before it passes an infielder excluding the pitcher, unless in the umpire's judgement, no infielder had a chance to play the ball

k. When a runner internationally kicks a ball which an infielder has missed.

The ball is dead and the baserunner is out. No bases may be run unless necessitated by the batter becoming a baserunner.

l. When the baserunner interferes with a fielder attempt in to field a batted ball or intentionally interferes with a thrown ball. If this interference, in the judgement of the umpire, is an obvious attempt to prevent a double play, the immediate succeeding runner shall also be called out.

m. When with a baserunner on third base, the batter interferes with a play being made a home plate worth less than two outs.

n. When anyone, other than another baserunner, physically assists a baserunner while the ball is in play.

o. When the coach near third base runs in the direction of home plate on or near the base line while a fielder is attempting to make a play on a batted or thrown ball and there by draws a throw to home plate. The baserunner nearest to third base shall be declared out.

p. When one or more members of the offensive team stand or collect at or around a base to which a baserunner is advancing thereby confusing the fielders and adding to the difficulty of making the play.

q. When the baserunner runs the base in reverse order to confuse the defensive team or to make a farce out of the game. This includes the batter-runner moving back toward home plate to avoid or delay a tag by a fielder.

r. If a coach intentionally interferes with a thrown ball.

s. When a runner, after being declared out or after scoring interferes with a defensive player's opportunity to make a play on another runner, the runner closest to home plate at the time of the interference, shall be declared out. The ball is dead and The baserunner is out other baserunner must return to the last base legally touched at the time of or before the illegal action.

t. When a defensive player has the ball and is waiting for the runner and the runner remains on his/her feet and deliberately, with great force, crashes into the defensive player, the runner is to be declared out.

The runner is out; the ball is dead and all other runners must return to the last base touched at the time of the collision.

u. When the baserunner fails to keep contact with the base to which he/she is entitled until a legally pitched ball has been released. When a baserunner is legitimately of his/her base after a pitch or the result of a batter completing his/her turn at bat, while the pitcher has the ball with in radius of the pitchers plate, he/she must immediately attempt to advance to the next base or immediately return to his/her base.

(1) Failure to immediately proceed to the next base or return to his/her base, once the pitcher has the ball with in the radius of the pitcher's plate shall result in the baserunner being declared out.

(2) Once the runner returns to a base for any reason he/she shall be declared out if he she/leave said base unless a play is made on him/her or another

runner (a fake throw is considered a play); or the pitcher no longer has possession of the ball within the radius; or the pitcher releases the ball by a pitch to the batter.

The ball is dead. No pitch is declared and the baserunner is out.

v. When he/she abandons a base, does not attempt to advance to the next base, and enters the team area or leaves the field of play. The baserunner shall be declared out immediately when he/she enters the team area or leaves the field of play.

Baserunners are not out under the following circumstances

a. When a baserunner runs behind the fielder and outside the baseline in order to avoid interfering with a fielder attempting to field the ball in the base path.

b. When a baserunner does not run in a direct line to the base providing the fielder in the direct line does not have the ball in his/her possession.

c. When more than one fielder attempts to field a batted ball and the baserunner comes in contact with the one who, in the umpire's judgement, was not entitled to field the ball.

d. When a baserunner is hit with a fair batted ball that has passed through an infielder, excluding the pitcher, and in the umpire's judgement, no other infielder, had a chance to make an out.

e. When a baserunner is touched with a ball not securely held by a fielder.

f. When the defensive team does not request the

umpire's decision on an appeal play until after the next pitch.

g. When a batter-baserunner passes first base after touching it and returns directly to the base.

h. When the baserunner is not given sufficient time to return to a base, he/she shall not be called out for being off base before the pitcher releases the ball He/She may advance as though he/she had left the base legally.

i. A runner who has legally started to advance cannot be stopped by the pitcher receiving the ball while on the pitching plate nor by stepping on the plate with the ball in his/her possession.

j. When a baserunner holds his/her base until a fly ball touches a fielder and then attempts to advance.

k. When hit by a batted ball when touching their base, unless they intentionally interfere with the ball or a fielder making a play.

i. When a baserunner slides into a base and dislodges it from its proper position, the base considered to have followed the runner.

A baserunner having made such base safely shall not be out for being off that base. He/She may return to that base without liability to be put out when the base has been replaced. A runner forfeits this exemption if he/she attempts to advance beyond the dislodged base before it is again in proper position.

m. When a fielder makes a play on a runner while using an illegal glove. The manager of the offended team has the option of having the entire play, including the batter's turn at bat, nullified, with the batter bating over, assuming the ball and strike count he/she had before he/she hit the ball and the runners returned to the original bases which the held prior to the batted ball or taking the result of the play.

n. When the baserunner is hit by a fair batted ball, after it is touched or touches any fielder, including the pitcher.

Dead Ball-ball in play

The ball is dead and not in play in the following circumstances:

a. When the ball is batted illegally.

b. When the batter steps from one box to another when the pitcher is ready to pitch.

If the pitcher completes the delivery of the ball to the batter and the batter hits the ball, reaches first base safely and all baserunners advance at least one base, then the play stands and the pitch is no longer illegal.

d. When 'No Pitch" is declared.

e. When a pitched ball touches any part of the batter's person or clothing whether the ball is struck at or not.

f. When foul ball in not caught.

g. When a baserunner is called out for leaving the base too soon on a pitched ball.

h. When the offensive team causes the interference:

(1) When a batter intentionally strikes the ball a second time, strikes it with a thrown bat, or deflects its course in any way while running to first base.

(2) When a thrown ball is intentionally touched by a coach.

(3) When a fair ball strikes a baserunner or umpire before touching an infielder including the pitcher or before passing an infielder other than the pitcher.

(4) When the batter interferes with the catcher.

(5) When member of the offensive team interferes intentionally with a live ball.

(6) When a runner intentionally kicks a ball which a fielder has missed.

(7) When with a baserunner on third base, the batter interferes with the play being made at home plate with less than two outs.

i. When the ball is outside the established playing limits of the playing area. A ball is considered "outside the playing field" when it touches the ground person on the ground or object outside the playing area.

j. If an accident to a runner is such as to prevent him/her from proceeding to abase to which he/she is awarded, a substitute runner shall be permitted for the injured player.

k. In case of interference with batter or fielder.

l. When a wild pitch or passed ball goes under, over or through the backstop.

m. When time is called by the umpire

n. When any part of the batter's person is hit with his/her own batted ball when he/she is in the batter's box.

o. When a baserunner runs bases in reverse order either to confuse the fielders or to make a travesty of the game.

p. When the batter is hit by a pitched ball.

q. When in the judgement of the umpire, the coach touches or helps the runner physically to assist him/her to return or to leave a base or when the coach near the third base runs in the direction of home plate on or near the baseline while the fielder is attempting to make a play on a batted or thrown ball and thereby drown a throw to home plate.

r. When there is interference by the plate umpire or his/her clothing with the catcher's attempt to throw.

s. When one or more members of the offensive team stand or collect at or around a base to which a baserunner is advancing, there by confusing the fielders and adding to the difficulty of making a play.

t. When the baserunner fails to keep contact with the base to which he/she is entitled until a legally pitched ball has been released.

u. When a play is being made on an obstructed runner or if the batter-runner is obstructed before he/she touches first base.

v. When a play is being made on an obstructed runner or if the batter-runner is obstructed before he/she touches first base.

v. When the catcher obstructs the batter's attempt to hit a pitch.

The ball remains alive if the batter reaches first base safely and all other runners have advanced at least one base.

w. When a blocked ball is declared.

x. When a batter enters the batter's box with or uses an altered bat.

y. When a batter hits a ball with an illegal bat.

z. When a caught fair fly ball (including a line drive) which can be handled by an infielder with ordinary effort is intentionally dropped with less than two outs and a runner on first base, first and second first and third, or first, second and third base.

ab. When a fielder intentionally carries a legally caught fly ball into dead ball territory.

Baserunners cannot advance on a dead ball, unless forced to do so by reason of the batter having reached first base as entitled to or they are awarded a base or bases.

The ball is in Play in the following circumstances

a. At the start of the game and each half inning when the pitcher has the ball while standing in his/her pitching position and the plate umpire has called "Play Ball."

b. When the ball becomes dead and it is apparent to the umpire that an appeal play is going to be made, it shall be put in play when the pitchers is within the radius of the pitcher's plate with the ball in his/her possession and the plate umpire call "Play Ball". The batter does not have to take his/her place in the batter's box on an apparent appeal play. However the players of the defensive team must take a position or fair territory with the exception of the catcher, who must be in the catcher's box.

c. When the infield fly rule is enforced.

d. When a thrown ball goes past a fielder and remains in playable territory.

e. When a fair ball strikes an umpire or baserunners on fair ground after passing or touching an infielder.

f. When a fair ball strikes an umpire on foul ground.

g. When the baserunners have reached the bases to which they are entitled when the fielder illegally fields a batted or thrown ball.

h. When a baserunner is called out for passing a preceding runner.

i. When no play is being made on an obstructed runner the ball shall remain alive until the play is over.

j. When a fair ball is legally batted.

k. When a baserunner acquires the right to a base by touching it before being put out.

m. When a base is dislodged while baserunners are progressing around the bases.

n. When a baserunner runs more than 1.0 m (3 ft.) from a direct line between a base and the next one in regular or reverse order to avoid being touched by the ball in the hand of a fielder.

o. When a baserunner is tagged or forced out.

p. When the umpire calls the baserunner out for failure to return and touch the base when play is resumed after a suspension of play.

q. When an appeal play is legally being made.

r. When the batter hits the ball.

s. When a live ball strikes a photographer, groundskeeper, policeman, etc.

t. When a fly ball has been legally caught

u. When a thrown ball strikes an offensive player.

v. If the batter drops the bat and the ball rolls against the bat in fair territory and in the umpire's judgement, there was no intention to interfere with the course of the ball, the batter is not out and the ball is alive and in play.

w. When a thrown ball strikes a coach.

x. Whenever the ball is not dead as provided in Section 1 of this rule.

y. When a thrown ball strikes a coach.

z. When a ball has been called on the batter and when foul balls have been called but the batter may not be put out before he/she reaches first base.

INDEX

Amateur Softball Association, 5

Baseball, 11

Class instruction, exercise for, 114
- bull-ups, 114
- bent knee sit-ups, 115
- modified push-ups, 115
- shuttle run, 115
- flexibility, 115
- endurance, 116

Competitive teams, exercise for, 116
- strength, 116
- agility, 117
- endurance, 118
- weight training, 119

Class organisation, structural, 122
- safety, 122
- instructional techniques, 124
- audio-visual aids, 124
- student leaders, 125
- environment condition, 125

Equipment, care of, 9
- gloves, 9
- balls, 9
- bats, 9
- shoes, 10

Infield skills, improving of, 85
- drills, 89
- force play, 89
- stationary ball, 89
- multiple-ball box drill, 90
- triple, 92

Modified softball, games of, 129
- hit pin softball, 130
- peggy, 131
- team pepper, 131
- one-pitch softball, 132
- co-recreational softball, 133

Softball, techniques of, 11
- pitching, 11
- stance, 11
- delivery, 12
- release, 13

Softball, skill tests of, 17
- equipment, 17
- description, 17
- scoring, 18, 20
- underhand pitching, 19
- speed throw, 19
- fungo hitting, 20
- base running, 21
- fielding ground balls, 21
- catching fly balls, 22
- repeated throws, 23
- batting pitched balls, 24

Softball, fundamental skills of, 27
- cognitive objectives, 29
- catching without glove, 31
- strategy of, 34
- common errors, 36
- overhand throw, 30

fielding grounds balls, 40
drills, 42
fielding fly balls, 47
backing up, 50
coursing, 52
double play, 53
relay, 55
defensive positions, 58
second baseman, 60
short stop, 61
third baseman, 62
catcher, 63
outfield, 65
offensive skills, 66
base running, 71

Softball coach, responsibility of, 136
scheduling, 136
contracting, 136
obtaining travel permits of, 136
budgeting, 137
procuring officials, 137
team selecting, 137
conducting try outs, 138
team meeting, 138
public relations, 139
mentally preparing, 139
conducting practice sessions, 140
staffing, 141
conducting warm-ups, 143
pre-game batting, 143
pre-game infield warm-up, 143
determining line-up, 145

Softball, rules/regulations of, 148
official softball, 148
playing field, 159
equipment, 161
warm-up bats, 162
player/substitutes, 164
designated hitter, 165
pitching regulation, 171
batting, 177
dead ball, 202

Teaching advanced, skills of, 77
advance throwing, 77
fast-pitch pitching, 81
infield, 83
cut off, 87
out field, 95
batting, 98
place hitting, 104
base running, 105
hit-and-run, 108
teaching tips, 109
stealing, 109